Windows 7 Configuration

Lab Manual

WILEY

EXECUTIVE EDITOR	John Kane
EDITORIAL PROGRAM ASSISTANT	Jennifer Lartz
DIRECTOR OF SALES	Mitchell Beaton
DIRECTOR OF MARKETING	Chris Ruel
SENIOR PRODUCTION AND MANUFACTURING MANAGER	Micheline Frederick
SENIOR PRODUCTION EDITOR	Kerry Weinstein

To order books or for customer service, please call 1-800-CALL WILEY (225-5945).

ISBN   978-0-470-87510-0

Printed in the United States of America

10 9 8 7 6

BRIEF CONTENTS

CONTENTS

LAB 1
UPGRADING TO WINDOWS 7

This lab contains the following exercises and activities:

Exercise 1.1   Running Upgrade Advisor

Exercise 1.2   Upgrading Windows Vista to Windows 7

BEFORE YOU BEGIN

The lab environment consists of student workstations connected to a local area network, along with a server that functions as the domain controller for a domain called contoso.com. The computers required for this lab are listed in Table 1-1.

Table 1-1
Computers required for Lab 1

Computer	Operating System	Computer Name
Server	Windows Server 2008 R2	RWDC01
Workstation 1	Windows Vista Enterprise SP1	NYC-CLa
Workstation 2	Windows Vista Enterprise SP1	NYC-CLb

In a classroom lab environment, there will be one classroom server and the students will have workstations named using consecutive numbers in place of the a and b variables. In a virtual lab environment, each student will have three virtual machines, named RWDC01, NYC-CL1, and NYC-CL2.

In addition to the computers, you will also require the software listed in Table 1-2 to complete Lab 1.

Table 1-2
Software required for Lab 1

Software	Location
Windows 7 Upgrade Advisor	\\rwdc01\downloads\Windows7UpgradeAdvisorSetup.exe
Windows 7 Enterprise installation files	\\rwdc01\downloads\win7ent
Lab 1 student worksheet	Lab01_worksheet.rtf (provided by instructor)

Working with Lab Worksheets

Each lab in this manual requires that you answer questions, provide screen shots, and perform other activities that you will document in a worksheet named for the lab, such as Lab01_worksheet.rtf. Your instructor will provide you with access to the worksheets. It is recommended that you use a USB flash drive to store your worksheets, so that you can submit them to your instructor for review. As you perform the exercises in each lab, open the appropriate worksheet file using WordPad, fill in the required information, and save the file to your flash drive.

SCENARIO

You are an IT manager making your first evaluations of the Windows 7 operating system. Your network consists of a large number of Windows Vista Enterprise workstations, and you want to determine whether it is feasible to upgrade them to Windows 7.

After completing this lab, you will be able to:

- Run the Windows 7 Upgrade Advisor application

- Upgrade a Windows Vista workstation to Windows 7

Estimated lab time: 50 minutes

Exercise 1.1	Running Upgrade Advisor
Overview	In Exercise 1.1, you run the Windows 7 Upgrade Advisor program on a Windows Vista computer to determine whether it is capable of running Windows 7.
Completion time	10 minutes

1. Turn on your Windows Vista workstation.

2. Press Ctrl+Alt+Del. The Windows logon page appears.

3. Click Switch User, and then click the Other User icon. In the User Name text box, type **contoso\Administrator**. In the Password text box, type **Pa$$w0rd**. Then click the right arrow button to log on.

4. Click Start, and in the Start Search box, type **\\rwdc01\downloads\Windows7UpgradeAdvisorSetup** and press Enter.

5. The *Welcome to the Windows 7 Upgrade Advisor Setup Wizard* page appears.

6. Select the *I accept the license terms* radio button and click Install. The *Installation complete* page appears.

7. Click Close.

8. Click Start. Then click All Programs > Windows 7 Upgrade Advisor. The Windows 7 Upgrade Advisor program loads, and the *Check to see if your PC is ready for Windows 7* page appears, as shown in Figure 1-1.

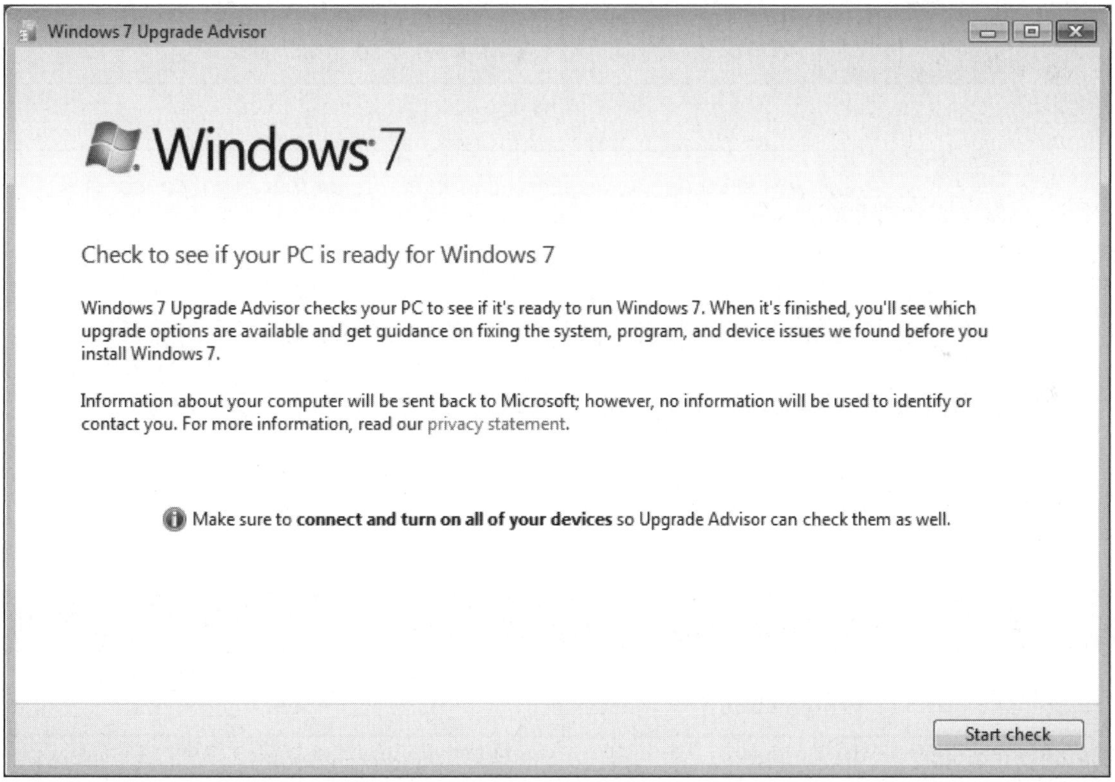

Figure 1-1
The *Check to see if your PC is ready for Windows 7* page

9. Click *Start Check*. The *Checking compatibility* page appears, and as the program scans the hardware and the software on the computer, it displays information about Windows 7.

10. When the result page appears, the program specifies whether your computer is capable of running Windows 7 and lists any issues you might need to address before you perform the upgrade.

11. Open your Lab01_worksheet file in WordPad and answer the following questions:

Question 1	*According to Upgrade Advisor, is your workstation capable of running Windows Vista?*

Question 2	*Is your workstation capable of running Windows Aero? If not, why not?*

Question 3	*Are there any devices in the computer for which Upgrade Advisor could not find information? If so, which ones?*

Question 4	*Are there any applications on the computer that might cause compatibility issues with Windows 7?*

12. Take a screen shot of the page that specifies whether the computer can run Windows 7 by pressing Alt+Prt Scr and then paste it into your Lab01_worksheet file in the page provided by pressing Ctrl+V.

13. Close the worksheet file, saving your work to your USB flash drive.

14. Leave the workstation logged on for the next exercise.

Exercise 1.2	Upgrading Windows Vista to Windows 7
Overview	In Exercise 1.2, you upgrade your Windows Vista workstation to Windows 7.
Completion time	40 minutes

NOTE	*In a classroom lab environment, students should choose partners and upgrade only one of their two Windows Vista workstations to Windows 7. The students will then use both workstations to migrate user profiles in Lab 2. In a virtual lab environment, each student should upgrade one of the two virtual workstations to Windows 7.*

1.   On your NYC-CLa workstation, click Start, and in the Start Search box, type **\\rwdc01\downloads\win7ent\setup** and press Enter. The *Install Windows* screen appears.

2.   Click Install Now. The *Get important updates for installation* page appears.

3.   Click Do not get the latest updates for installation. The *Please read the license terms* page appears.

4.   Select the I accept the license terms check box and click Next. The *Which type of installation do you want?* page appears.

5.   Click Upgrade. After a compatibility check, a Compatibility Report screen appears, listing any problems or potential problems with the computer's hardware or software configuration.

6.   Click Next. The *Upgrading Windows* page appears. After a period that can last 30 minutes or more during which the setup program installs Windows 7, the computer reboots and the *Type your Windows product key* page appears.

7.   Click Next. The *Help protect your computer and improve Windows automatically* page appears.

8.   Click Ask me later. The *Review your time and date settings* page appears.

9.   From the *Time zone* drop-down list, select your time zone and, if necessary, correct the Date and Time settings. Click Next. A *Thank You* page appears.

10.   Click Start. The Windows logon page appears.

11.   Press Ctrl+Alt+Del and log on to Windows 7 using the **contoso\Administrator** user name and the password **Pa$$w0rd**. Windows 7 loads.

12.   Shut down the workstation computer.

LAB 2
MIGRATING USER PROFILES

This lab contains the following exercises and activities:

Exercise 2.1	Creating User Profiles
Exercise 2.2	Installing Windows Easy Transfer on Windows Vista
Exercise 2.3	Collecting User Profile Data
Exercise 2.4	Importing User Profile Data
Exercise 2.5	Testing User Profiles
Lab Challenge 2.1	Migrating User Profiles over the Network

BEFORE YOU BEGIN

The lab environment consists of student workstations connected to a local area network, along with a server that functions as the domain controller for a domain called contoso.com. The computers required for this lab are listed in Table 2-1.

Table 2-1
Computers required for Lab 2

Computer	Operating System	Computer Name
Server	Windows Server 2008 R2	RWDC01
Workstation 1	Windows 7 Enterprise	NYC-CLa
Workstation 2	Windows Vista Enterprise SP1 or higher	NYC-CLb

NOTE

In a classroom lab environment, there will be one classroom server and the students will have workstations named using consecutive numbers in place of the a and b variables. In a virtual lab environment, each student will have three virtual machines, named RWDC01, NYC-CL1, and NYC-CL2.

In addition to the computers, you will also require the software listed in Table 2-2 to complete Lab 2.

Table 2-2
Software required for Lab 2

Software	Location
Windows Easy Transfer for transferring from Windows Vista (32-bit) to Windows 7	\\rwdc01\downloads\Windows6.0-KB928635-x86.msu
Lab 2 student worksheet	Lab02_worksheet.rtf (provided by instructor)

Working with Lab Worksheets

Each lab in this manual requires that you answer questions, take screen shots, and perform other activities that you will document in a worksheet named for the lab, such as Lab02_worksheet.rtf. Your instructor will provide you with access to the worksheets. It is recommended that you use a USB flash drive to store your worksheets, so that you can submit them to your instructor for review. As you perform the exercises in each lab, open the appropriate worksheet file using WordPad, fill in the required information, and save the file to your flash drive.

SCENARIO

A user calls the help desk for assistance because she is running two computers, one with Windows 7 and one with Windows Vista. She originally requested Windows 7 on her new computer to test the new operating system herself, but now her office mates, who share the computers, are interested in trying Windows 7 as well. Your user wants to transfer the other users' accounts and documents from Windows Vista to

Windows 7 so that they can each log on using their own names. However, the user explains that there is only one network jack in the room, so it is only possible to connect one computer at a time. You explain to her that she can use the Windows Easy Transfer utility to do this.

After completing this lab, you will be able to:

- Create new accounts with user profiles

- Install Windows Easy Transfer on a Windows Vista computer

- Use Windows Easy Transfer to gather user profile information

- Use Windows Easy Transfer to migrate user profile information from one operating system to another

Estimated lab time: 70 minutes

Exercise 2.1	Creating User Profiles
Overview	In Exercise 2.1, you create and populate additional user profiles on your Windows Vista installation in preparation for transferring them to Windows 7 using Windows Easy Transfer.
Completion time	10 minutes

> NOTE
>
> *In a classroom lab environment, students should work with a partner so that they have one workstation running Windows Vista SP1 and one workstation that has been upgraded to Windows 7. In a virtual lab environment, each student will have three virtual machines, named RWDC01, NYC-CL1, and NYC-CL2.*

1. Turn on NYC-CLb, your Windows Vista workstation, and log on using the **contoso\Administrator** account and the password **Pa$$w0rd**.

2. Click Start, and then click Control Panel > System and Maintenance > Administrative Tools. The Administrative Tools control panel appears.

3. Double click Computer Management. The Computer Management console appears.

4. Expand the Local Users and Groups node and select the Users container.

5. Right click the Users container and, from the context menu, select New User. The New User dialog box appears, as shown in Figure 2-1.

Figure 2-1
The New User dialog box

6. In the User name text box, type **Alice**.

7. In the Password and Confirm password text boxes, type **Pa$$w0rd**.

8. Clear the *User must change password at next logon* check box and click Create. The system creates the user account and presents a blank new User dialog box.

9. Repeat steps 6 to 8 to create three additional user accounts called Ralph, Ed, and Trixie.

10. Click Close. The four new accounts appear in the Users container.

11. Click Start, and then click the right-arrow button and select Log Off from the context menu. The system logs off of the current account.

12. Press Ctrl+Alt+Delete and then click Switch User.

13. Click Other User and log on using the **NYC-CLb\Alice** account you just created, with the password **Pa$$w0rd**.

14. Repeat steps 11 to 13 to log off and log on again, using the **NYC-CLb\Ed** account you just created and the password **Pa$$w0rd**.

15. Log off of the workstation.

Exercise 2.2	Installing Windows Easy Transfer on Windows Vista
Overview	In Exercise 2.2, you install Windows Easy Transfer on the Windows Vista computer.
Completion time	5 minutes

1. Log on to the NYC-CLb Windows Vista workstation using the **contoso\ Administrator** account and the password **Pa$$w0rd**.

2. Click Start, and in the Start Search text box, type **\\rwdc01\downloads\ Windows6.0-KB928635-x86.msu** and press Enter. A Windows Update Standalone Installer message box appears.

3. Click OK. The Read these license terms dialog box appears.

4. Click *I accept*. The Installer program installs Windows Easy Transfer.

5. Click Close.

6. Leave the computer logged on for the next exercise.

Exercise 2.3	Collecting User Profile Data
Overview	In Exercise 2.3, you run the Windows Easy Transfer program on Windows Vista and collect the user profile data you want to migrate to Windows 7.
Completion time	15 minutes

1. Click Start. Then click All Programs > Windows Easy Transfer for Windows 7. The Windows Easy Transfer Wizard appears, displaying the *Welcome to Windows Easy Transfer* page.

NOTE

Be sure to run the version of Windows Easy Transfer for Windows 7 you just installed, not the version included with Windows Vista. The Vista version is not capable of transferring user profile settings to a Windows 7 computer.

2. Click Next. The *What do you want to use to transfer items to your new computer?* page appears.

3. Click *An external hard disk or USB flash drive*. The *Which computer are you using now?* page appears.

4. Click *This is my old computer*. The program scans the computer for files and settings it can transfer and displays the results in the *Choose what to transfer from this computer* page, as shown in Figure 2-2.

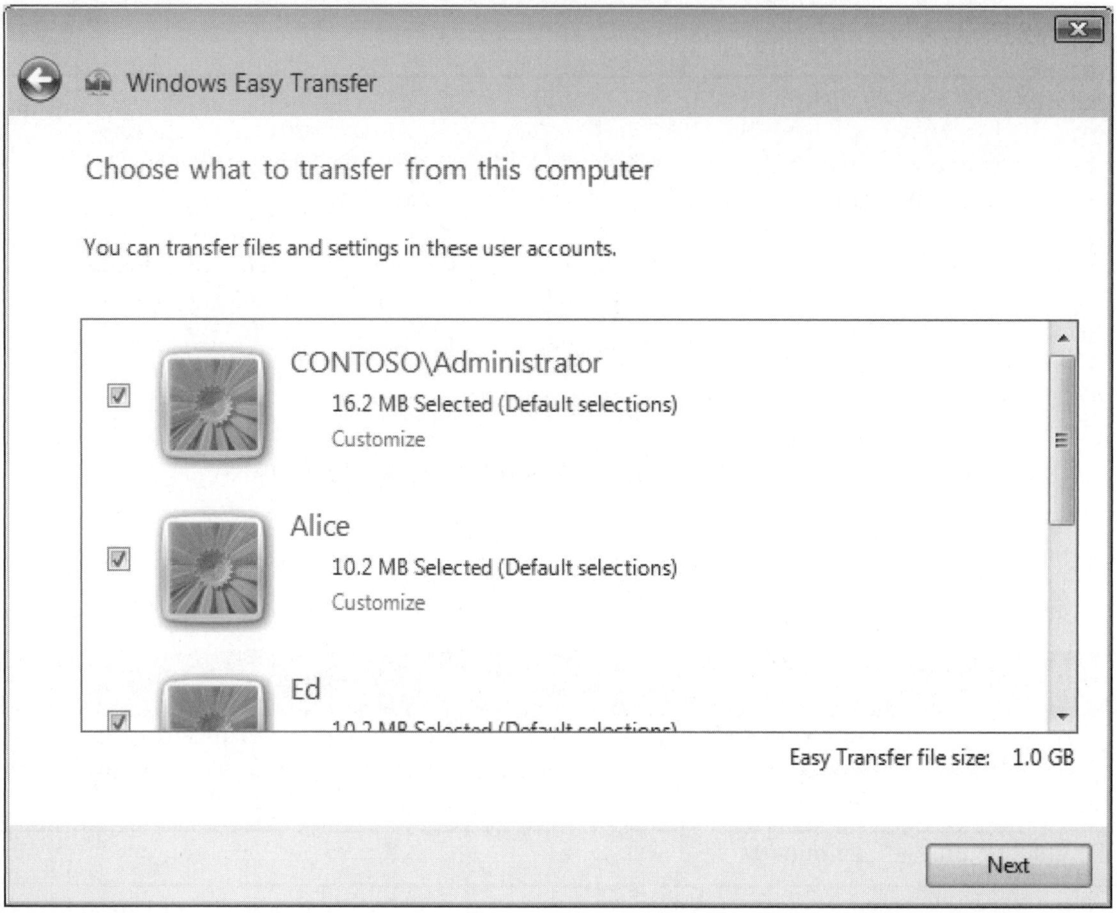

Figure 2-2
The *Choose what to transfer from this computer* page

Question 1	*Which user profiles are available for transfer?*

5. Select the check boxes for all of the available accounts and the Shared Items object and click Next. The *Save your files and settings for transfer* page appears.

Question 2	*Why aren't the user profiles for all of the accounts you created available for transfer?*

6.   In the Password and Confirm password text boxes, type **Pa$$w0rd** and click Save. The *Save your Easy Transfer file* combo box appears.

7.   In the File name text box, type **\\rwdc01\downloads\eastNYC-CLb** (where b is the number of your workstation) and click Save. The wizard saves the selected settings to the lab server, and then displays a *These files and settings have been saved for your transfer* page.

8.   Click Next. The *Your transfer file is complete* page appears, as shown in Figure 2-3. The page displays the filename you specified and the location where you saved it.

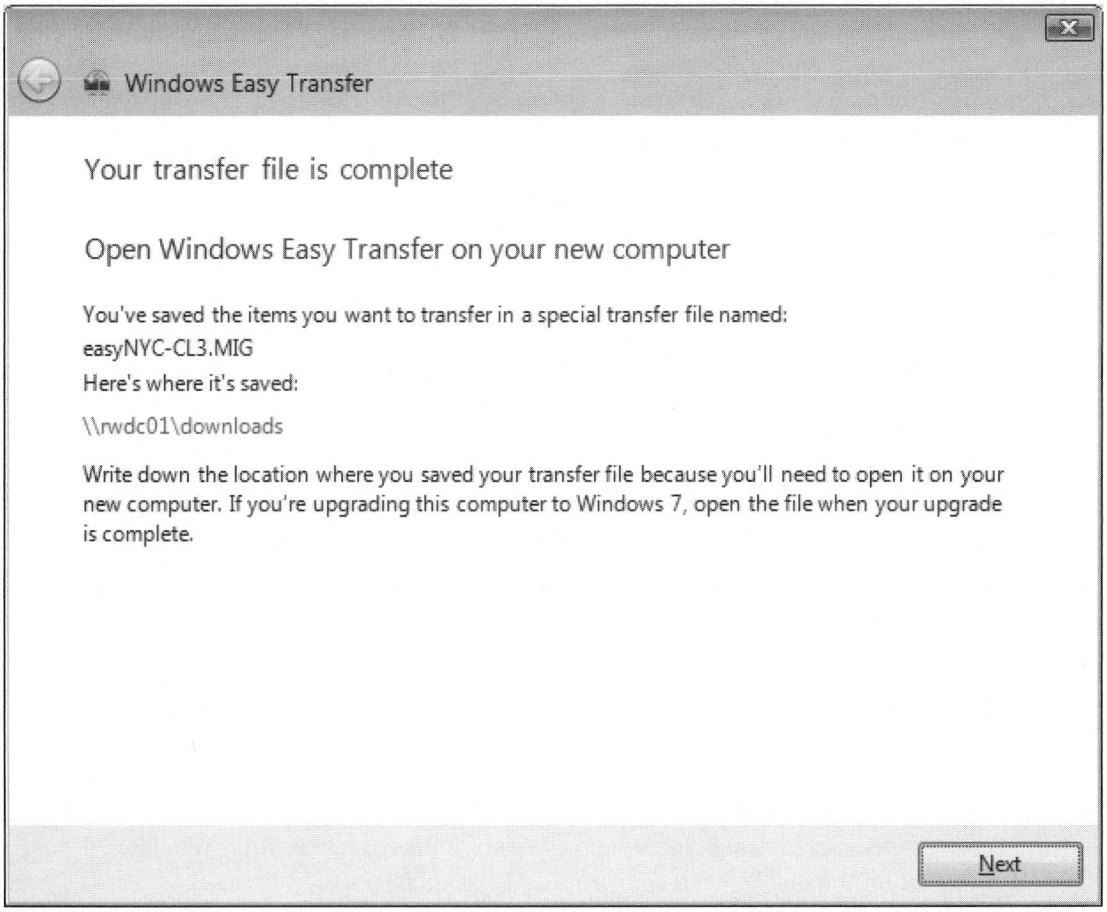

Figure 2-3
The *Your transfer file is complete* page

9.   Click Next. The *Windows Easy Transfer is complete on this computer* page appears.

10. Click Close. The wizard closes.

11. Shut down your Windows Vista workstation.

Exercise 2.4	Importing User Profile Data
Overview	In Exercise 2.4, you import the user profile data you collected in the previous exercise into Windows 7.
Completion time	15 minutes

1. On your partner's workstation, already upgraded to Windows 7, log on using the **contoso\Administrator** account and the password **Pa$$w0rd**.

2. Click Start. Then click All Programs > Accessories > System Tools > Windows Easy Transfer. The *Welcome To Windows Easy Transfer* page appears again.

3. Click Next. The *What do you want to use to transfer items to your new computer?* page appears.

4. Click *An external hard disk or USB flash drive*. The *Which computer are you using now?* page appears.

5. Click *This is my new computer*. The *Has Windows Easy Transfer already saved your files from your old computer to an external hard disk or USB flash drive?* page appears.

6. Click Yes. The Open an Easy Transfer file combo box appears.

7. In the File name text box, type **\\rwdc01\downloads\eastNYC-CLb.MIG** (where b is the number of your workstation) and click Open. The *Enter the password you used to help protect your transfer file and start the transfer* page appears.

8. In the text box, type **Pa$$w0rd** and click Next. The wizard opens the file and displays the *Choose what to transfer to this computer* page, as shown in Figure 2-2.

9. Select all of the available items and click Transfer. The wizard transfers the settings you saved from the Windows Vista workstation to your Windows 7 workstation and displays the *Your transfer is complete* page.

10. Click *See what was transferred*. The Windows Easy Transfer Reports window appears.

11. Take a screen shot of the Windows Easy Transfer Reports window by pressing Alt+Prt Scr and then paste it into your Lab02_worksheet file in the page provided by pressing Ctrl+V.

12. Close the Windows Easy Transfer Reports window.

13. Click Close. A Restart your computer to complete your transfer dialog box appears.

14. Click Restart now. The Windows 7 workstation restarts.

Exercise 2.5	Testing User Profiles
Overview	In Exercise 2.5, you examine the data that Windows Easy Transfer has migrated to Windows 7 and test the new user profiles that the application has created.
Completion time	10 minutes

1. Press Ctrl+Alt+Delete and log on using the NYC-CLb\Ed account and the password **Pa$$w0rd**.

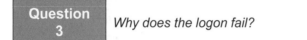

Question 3	Why does the logon fail?

2. Try again to log on using the NYC-CLb\Ed account, this time with no password. An error message appears, stating that the user's password must be changed before logging on for the first time.

3. Click OK. A password change window appears.

4. Leave the Password text box blank, and in the New password and Confirm password text boxes, type **Pa$$w0rd** and click the right-arrow button. A message appears, stating that the password has been changed.

5. Click OK. The system completes Ed's logon.

6. Log off and try to log on using the Ralph account you created in Exercise 2.1.

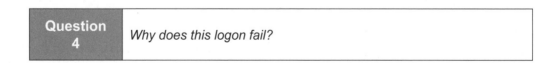

Question 4	Why does this logon fail?

7. Log on using the Alice account you created, changing the password to **Pa$$w0rd** as needed.

Question 5	Is the Alice logon successful?

8. Shut down the workstation.

LAB CHALLENGE 2.1: MIGRATING USER PROFILES OVER THE NETWORK

Completion time	15 minutes

Another user in the company wants to transfer user profiles from a Windows Vista workstation to a Windows 7 workstation, but these two computers are both connected to the network at the same time. To complete this challenge, you and your partner must create two new local user accounts on the Windows Vista workstation and transfer them directly to the Windows 7 workstation, using the network. Then complete the following tasks:

1. Write out the steps you performed to complete the challenge.

2. Take a screen shot as the user profile transfer is occurring by pressing Alt+Prt Scr and then paste it into your Lab02_worksheet file in the page provided by pressing Ctrl+V.

LAB 3
INSTALLING
WINDOWS 7

This lab contains the following exercises and activities:

Exercise 3.1   Installing Windows 7 from a DVD

Exercise 3.2   Joining a Workstation to a Domain

BEFORE YOU BEGIN

The lab environment consists of student workstations connected to a local area network, along with a server that functions as the domain controller for a domain called contoso.com. The computers required for this lab are listed in Table 3-1.

Table 3-1
Computers required for Lab 3

Computer	Operating System	Computer Name
Server	Windows Server 2008 R2	RWDC01
Workstation 1	None	NYC-CLa

In a classroom lab environment, there will be one classroom server and the students will have workstations named using consecutive numbers in place of the a and b variables. In a virtual lab environment, each student will have three virtual machines, named RWDC01, NYC-CL1, and NYC-CL2.

In addition to the computers, you will also require the software listed in Table 3-2 to complete Lab 3.

Table 3-2
Software required for Lab 3

Software	Location
Windows 7 Enterprise installation files	DVD (provided by instructor)
Lab 3 student worksheet	Lab03_worksheet.rtf (provided by instructor)

Working with Lab Worksheets

Each lab in this manual requires that you answer questions, shoot screen shots, and perform other activities that you will document in a worksheet named for the lab, such as Lab03_worksheet.rtf. Your instructor will provide you with access to the worksheets. It is recommended that you use a USB flash drive to store your worksheets, so that you can submit them to your instructor for review. As you perform the exercises in each lab, open the appropriate worksheet file using WordPad, fill in the required information, and save the file to your flash drive.

SCENARIO

A user calls the help desk for assistance because she has completed the process of transferring user profiles from her Windows Vista workstation to her Windows 7 workstation. Now, she wants you to perform a clean Windows 7 installation on the Vista workstation, removing all traces of the old operating system.

After completing this lab, you will be able to:

■   Perform a clean installation of Windows 7 from a DVD

■   Join a newly installed workstation to an Active Directory Domain Services domain

Estimated lab time: 25 minutes

Exercise 3.1	Installing Windows 7 from a DVD
Overview	In Exercise 3.1, you install Windows 7 on a workstation, using a standard installation DVD.
Completion time	20 minutes

> NOTE *In a classroom lab environment, each student should install (or reinstall) Windows 7 on his or her own workstation, regardless of its current status. This is to ensure a clean working environment for subsequent labs.*

1. Turn on the computer and immediately insert the Windows 7 installation disk into the DVD drive.

2. Press any key to boot from the DVD (if necessary). A progress indicator screen appears as Windows is loading files.

3. The computer switches to the Windows graphical interface and the *Install Windows* page appears, as shown in Figure 3-1.

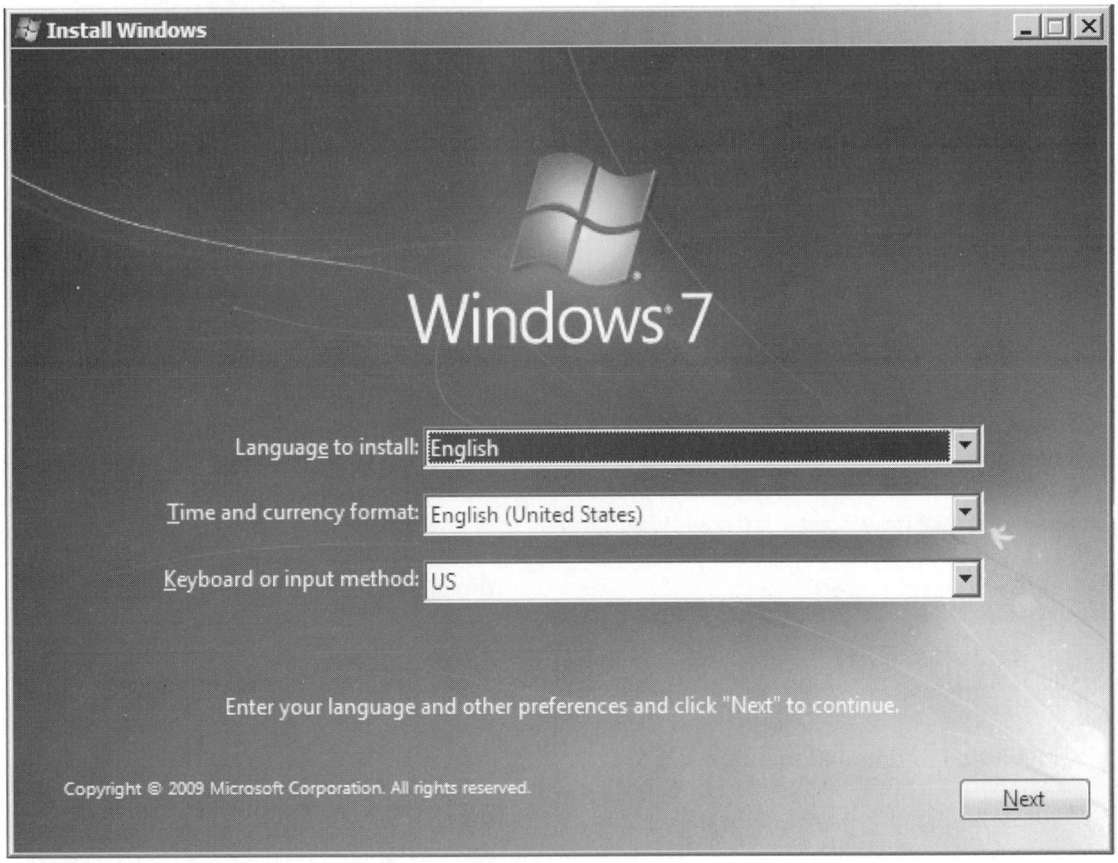

Figure 3-1
The *Install Windows* page

4. Click Next to accept the default values for the *Language to install*, *Time and currency format*, and *Keyboard or input method* parameters. The *Install now* screen appears.

5. Click Install now. The *Please read the license terms* page appears.

6. Select the *I accept the license terms* check box and click Next. The *Which type of installation do you want?* page appears.

7. Click the *Custom (advanced)* option. The *Where do you want to install Windows?* page appears, as shown in Figure 3-2.

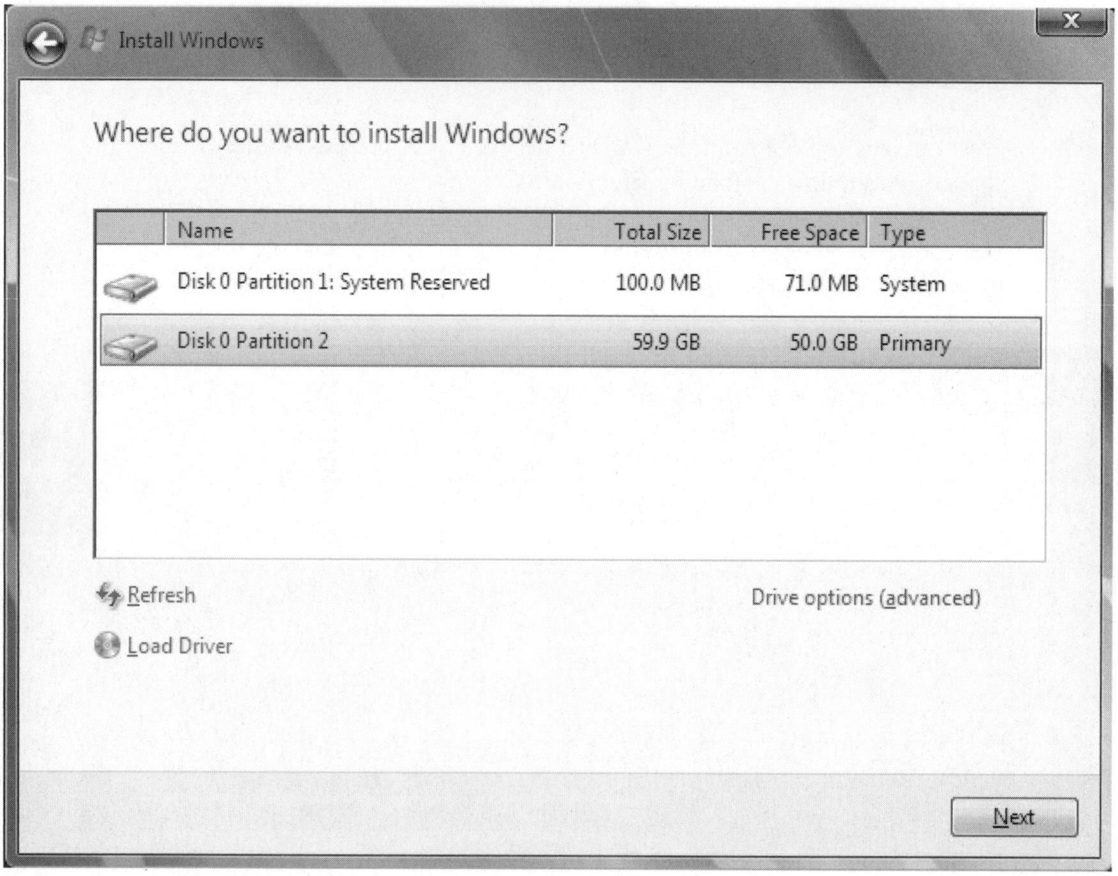

Figure 3-2
The *Where do you want to install Windows?* page

8. Click Drive options (advanced). Additional command buttons for manipulating the drives appear.

9. Select a partition in the list and click Delete. A warning box appears, prompting you to confirm that you want to delete the partition.

10. Click OK. The system deletes the partition.

11. Repeat steps 9 and 10, if necessary, to delete all other existing partitions on the computer.

12. Click New. The new partition controls appear.

13. In the Size spin box, specify a size of at least 20 GB, leaving another 20 GB of unpartitioned space on the computer.

14. Click Apply. A message box appears, specifying that Windows might have to create additional partitions.

15. Click OK. The system creates the partition you defined, as well as a 100 MB partition, as shown in Figure 3-3.

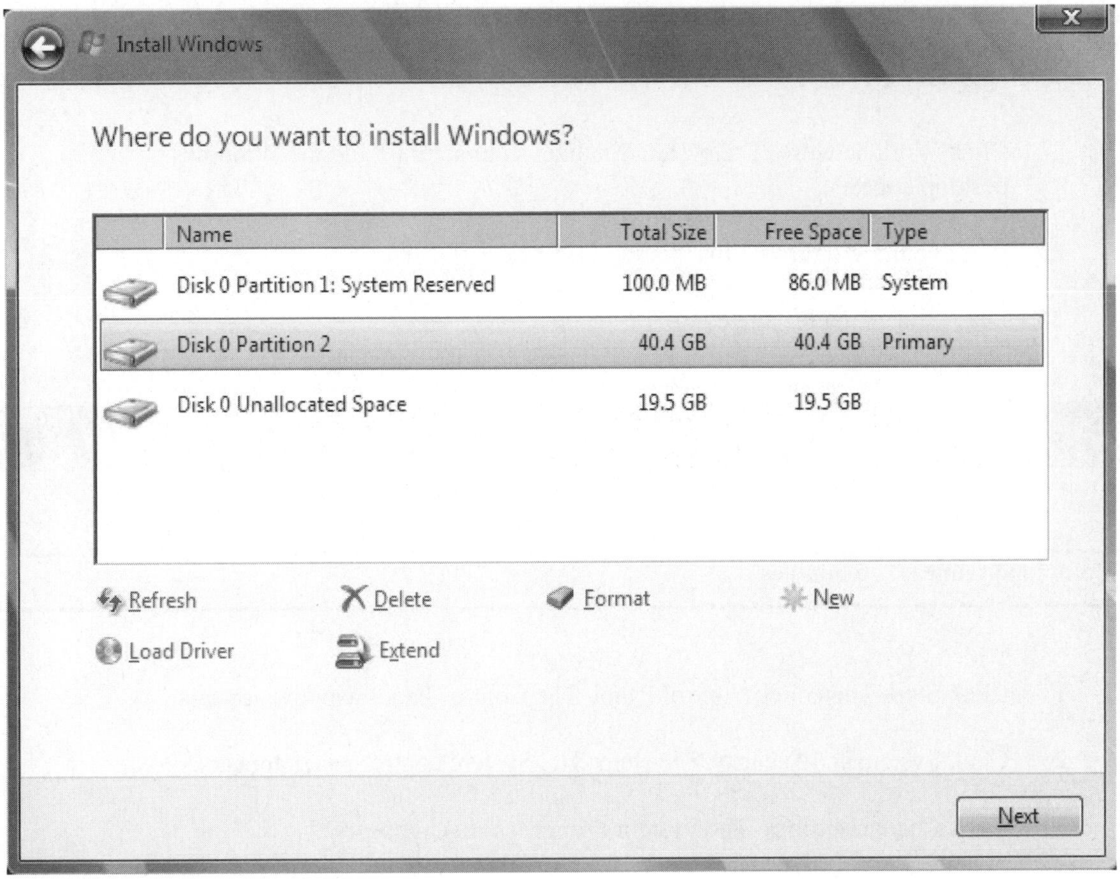

Figure 3-3
New partitions on the *Where do you want to install Windows?* page

Question 1	What types of partitions did the system create?

16. Select the larger partition you just created and click Next. The system installs Windows 7, a process that takes several minutes and requires two system restarts. Then the *Set Up Windows* page appears.

17. In the *Type a user name* text box, type **student**.

18. In the *Type a computer name* text box, type **NYC-CLa**, where a is the original number of your workstation, and click Next. The *Set a password for your account* page appears.

19. In the three text boxes, type **Pa$$w0rd** and click Next. The *Help protect your computer and improve Windows automatically* page appears.

20. Click Ask me later. The *Review your time and date settings* page appears.

21. From the *Time zone* drop-down list, select the correct time zone for your location. If the date and time specified in the calendar and clock are not accurate, correct the settings and click Next. The *Select your computer's current location* page appears.

22. Click Work network. The system finalizes your settings and the Windows desktop appears.

23. Remove the Windows 7 installation DVD from the drive.

24. Leave the computer logged on for the next exercise.

Exercise 3.2	Joining a Workstation to a Domain
Overview	In Exercise 3.2, you join your newly installed Windows 7 workstation to your network's Active Directory Domain Services domain.
Completion time	5 minutes

1. Click Start. Then click Control Panel. The Control Panel window appears.

2. Click System and Security > System. The System control panel appears.

3. Click Change settings. The System Properties sheet appears.

4. Click Change. The Computer Name/Domain Changes dialog box appears, as shown in Figure 3-4.

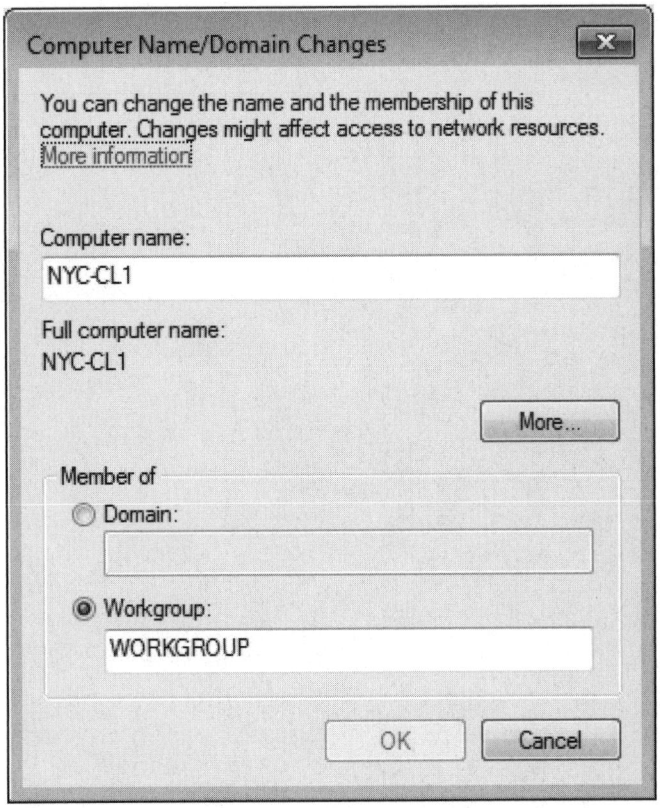

Figure 3-4
The Computer Name/Domain Changes dialog box

5. Select the *Domain* option, and type **contoso** in the text box. Then click OK. A
    Windows Security dialog box appears.

6. Authenticate with the user name **Administrator** and the password **Pa$$w0rd**
    and click OK. A message box appears, welcoming you to the domain.

7. Take a screen shot of the message box by pressing Alt+Prt Scr and paste it into
    your Lab03_worksheet file in the page provided by pressing Ctrl+V.

8. Click OK. Another message box appears, prompting you to restart the computer.

9. Click OK.

10. Click Close to close the System Properties dialog box.

11. A *You must restart your computer to apply these changes* message box appears.

12. Click Restart Now. The computer restarts.

LAB 4
CAPTURING A REFERENCE IMAGE

This lab contains the following exercises and activities:

Exercise 4.1   Installing Windows 7 AIK

Exercise 4.2   Creating an Answer File

Exercise 4.3   Creating a Windows PE Boot Image

Exercise 4.4   Capturing an Image

Lab Challenge 4.1   Creating a Capture Image

BEFORE YOU BEGIN

The lab environment consists of student workstations connected to a local area network, along with a server that functions as the domain controller for a domain called contoso.com. The computers required for this lab are listed in Table 4-1.

Table 4-1
Computers required for Lab 4

Computer	Operating System	Computer Name
Server	Windows Server 2008 R2	RWDC01
Workstation 1	Windows 7 Enterprise	NYC-CLa

NOTE	*In a classroom lab environment, there will be one classroom server and the students will have workstations named using consecutive numbers in place of the a and b variables. In a virtual lab environment, each student will have three virtual machines, named RWDC01, NYC-CL1, and NYC-CL2.*

In addition to the computers, you will also require the software listed in Table 4-2 to complete Lab 4.

Table 4-2
Software required for Lab 4

Software	Location
Windows 7 AIK installation files	\\rwdc01\downloads\win7aik
Windows PE boot disk	CD or DVD (provided by instructor)
Windows 7 Enterprise installation files	\\rwdc01\downloads\win7ent
Lab 4 student worksheet	Lab04_worksheet.rtf (provided by instructor)

Working with Lab Worksheets

Each lab in this manual requires that you answer questions, shoot screen shots, and perform other activities that you will document in a worksheet named for the lab, such as Lab04_worksheet.rtf. Your instructor will provide you with access to the worksheets. It is recommended that you use a USB flash drive to store your worksheets, so that you can submit them to your instructor for review. As you perform the exercises in each lab, open the appropriate worksheet file using WordPad, fill in the required information, and save the file to your flash drive.

SCENARIO

As part of the planning stage of a Windows 7 workstation deployment project, you have been assigned the task of installing the Windows 7 Automated Installation Kit, building a reference computer, and capturing an image of the reference computer.

After completing this lab, you will be able to:

- Install Windows 7 AIK

- Create a Windows PE boot disk

- Create an answer file using Windows System Information Manager

- Capture an image of a reference computer using ImageX.exe

Estimated lab time: 80 minutes

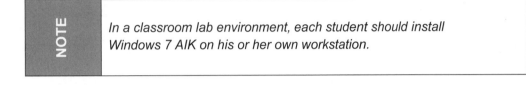

Exercise 4.1	Installing Windows 7 AIK
Overview	In Exercise 4.1, you install Windows 7 AIK on a workstation, using installation files stored on your server.
Completion time	10 minutes

> **NOTE**
>
> *In a classroom lab environment, each student should install Windows 7 AIK on his or her own workstation.*

1. Log on to NYC-CLa using the **contoso\Administrator** user account and the password **Pa$$w0rd**.

2. Click Start, and in the *Search programs and files* box, type **\\rwdc01\downloads\win7aik\startcd** and press Enter. The Welcome to Windows Automated Installation Kit window appears, as shown in Figure 4-1.

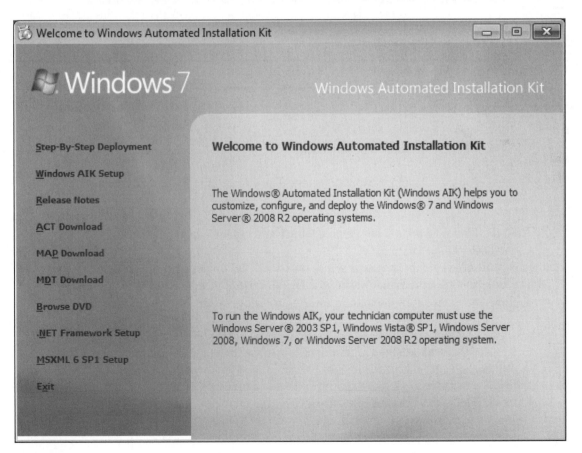

Figure 4-1
The Welcome to Windows Automated Installation Kit window

3. Click Windows AIK Setup. The Windows Automated Installation Kit Setup Wizard appears.

4. Click Next to bypass the *Welcome* page. The *License Terms* page appears.

5. Select the *I agree* option and click Next. The *Select Installation Folder* page appears.

6. Click Next to accept the default folder. The *Confirm Installation* page appears.

7. Click Next. The wizard installs the Windows 7 AIK, and then displays the *Installation Complete* page.

8. Click Close.

9. Close the Welcome to Windows Automated Installation Kit window.

10. Leave the workstation logged on for the next exercise.

Exercise 4.2	Creating an Answer File
Overview	In Exercise 4.2, you use the Windows System Image Manager to create an answer file that partitions a computer's disk during the Windows 7 installation procedure.
Completion time	15 minutes

1. Click Start. Then click All Programs > Microsoft Windows AIK > Windows System Image Manager. The Windows System Image Manager window appears.

2. Click Tools > Create Distribution Share. The Create Distribution Share combo box appears.

3. In the Folder name text box, type **c:\share** and click Open. The share appears in the Distribution Share pane.

4. Click File > Select Windows Image. The Select a Windows Image combo box appears.

5. In the File name text box, type **\\rwdc01\downloads\win7ent\sources\install.wim** and press Enter. The Windows 7 ENTERPRISE image appears in the Windows Image pane.

6. Click File > New Answer File. The answer file elements appear in the Answer File pane, as shown in Figure 4-2.

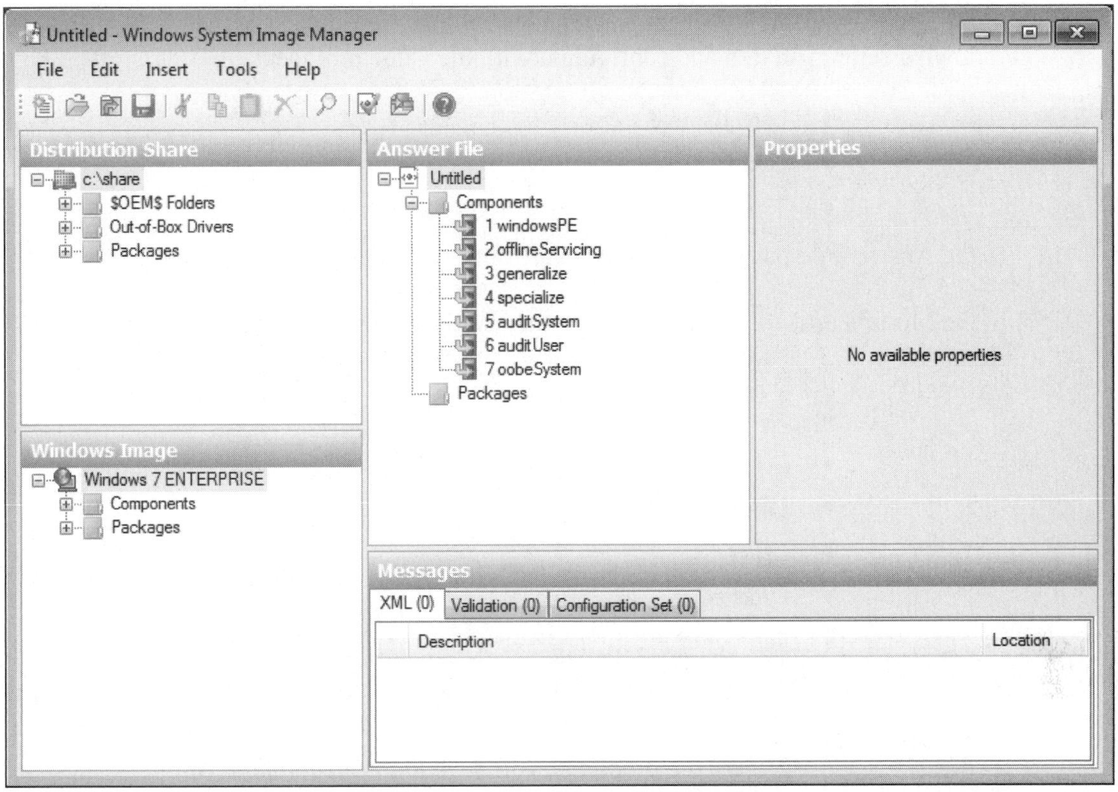

Figure 4-2
Creating an answer file in Windows System Image Manager

7. In the Windows Image pane, expand the Windows 7 ENTERPRISE\Components folder and browse to the amd64_Microsoft-Windows-Setup\DiskConfiguration\Disk\CreatePartitions\CreatePartition container.

8. Right click CreatePartition and, from the context menu, select *Add Setting to Pass 1 windowsPE*. The CreatePartition setting appears in the Answer File pane.

9. Expand the ModifyPartitions container, then right click ModifyPartition and, from the context menu, select *Add Setting to Pass 1 windowsPE*. The ModifyPartition setting appears in the Answer File pane.

10. In the Answer File box, select Disk.

11. In the Disk Properties pane, under Settings, select each of the following settings in turn and configure it with the value provided:

    - DiskID = 0
    - WillWipeDisk = true

12. In the Answer File pane, select CreatePartition.

13. In the CreatePartition Properties pane, under Settings, select each of the following settings in turn and configure it with the value provided:

    - Extend = true
    - Order = 1
    - Type = Primary

14. In the Answer File pane, select ModifyPartition.

15. In the ModifyPartition Properties box, under Settings, configure the following settings:

    - Active = true
    - Format = NTFS
    - Label = Windows
    - Letter = C
    - Order = 1
    - PartitionID = 1

Question 1	*What will the properties you have just configured do when you include them in an answer file that you use to install Windows 7?*

16. From the Tools menu, select Validate Answer File. The Messages box reads No Warnings or Errors.

17. Take a screen shot of the Windows System Image Manager window by pressing Alt+Prt Scr and paste it into your Lab04_worksheet file in the page provided by pressing Ctrl+V.

18. Click Tools > Create Configuration Set. The Create Configuration Set dialog box appears.

19. In the Select the target folder for the configuration set text box, type **c:\share\configset** and click OK.

20. A message box appears, prompting you to confirm that you want the program to create the folder.

21. Click Yes. The system creates the configuration set.

22. Another message box appears, confirming that the program has successfully created the configuration set.

23. Click OK.

24. Close the Windows System Image Manager window.

25. Leave the computer logged on for the next exercise.

Exercise 4.3	Creating a Windows PE Boot Image
Overview	In Exercise 4.3, you use the tools provided with Windows 7 AIK to create a Windows PE boot image.
Completion time	10 minutes

1. Click Start > All Programs > Microsoft Windows AIK. Then right click the Deployment Tools Command Prompt shortcut and, from the context menu, select Run as Administrator. An elevated command prompt window appears.

2. Run the Copype.cmd script using the following syntax:

    ```
    copype.cmd amd64 C:\winpe
    ```

    The script creates a directory structure at the specified location, as shown in Figure 4-3.

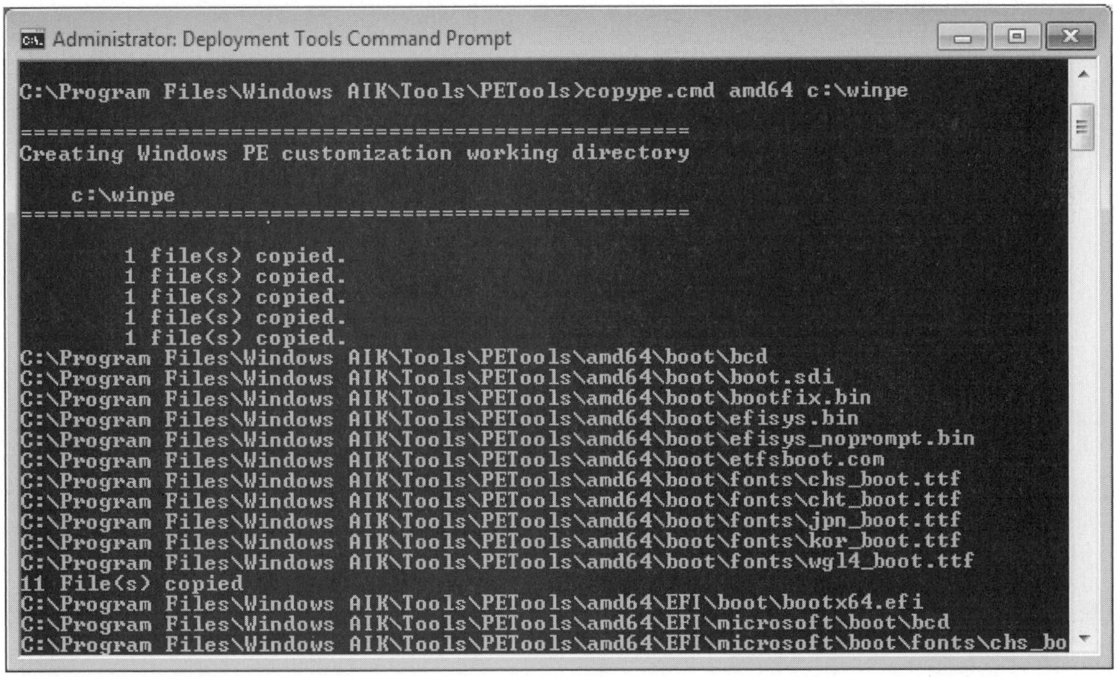

Figure 4-3
Running the Copype.cmd script

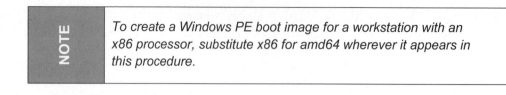

> **NOTE** To create a Windows PE boot image for a workstation with an x86 processor, substitute x86 for amd64 wherever it appears in this procedure.

3. Copy the boot image file (Winpe.wim) to the C:\Winpe\ISO\Sources folder and rename it, using the following command:

```
copy c:\winpe\winpe.wim
c:\winpe\ISO\sources\boot.wim
```

> **Question 2** How can you use the Boot.wim image file to boot a workstation into Windows PE?

4. Copy the ImageX.exe file to the c:\winpe\ISO folder, using the following command:

```
copy "c:\Program files\Windows
AIK\Tools\amd64\imagex.exe" c:\winpe\ISO
```

5. Package the Windows PE files into a sector-based image file (with an .iso extension) using the Oscdimg.exe program with the following syntax:

```
oscdimg.exe -n -bc:\winpe\etfsboot.com
c:\winpe\ISO c:\winpe\winpe.iso
```

6. Burn the Winpe.iso image you created to a CD-ROM or DVD-ROM, using the software provided with your drive.

>  **NOTE** Check with your instructor before you attempt to burn a disk. If your workstation is equipped with a CD or DVD burner, your instructor might supply you with a blank disk and a procedure for burning your own Windows PE boot disk. If your workstation is not properly equipped, your instructor might supply you with a boot disk or instructions on how to boot from the network.

7. Leave the computer logged on for the next exercise.

Exercise 4.4	Capturing an Image
Overview	In Exercise 4.4, you boot your workstation with the Windows PE disk you created and use the Image.exe program to capture an image of the workstation's drive.
Completion time	30 minutes

1. In the elevated command prompt window you opened in Exercise 4.3, switch to the Sysprep folder using the following command:

   cd\windows\system32\sysprep

2. Prepare the computer for imaging by running the Sysprep.exe program, using the following syntax:

   sysprep /generalize /oobe

   When Sysprep.exe finishes running, the computer shuts down.

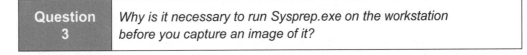

Question 3	Why is it necessary to run Sysprep.exe on the workstation before you capture an image of it?

3. Start the computer using the Windows PE boot disk you created in Exercise 4.3. The system boots to a command prompt.

4. Use the following command to map the Z: drive to your server:

   net use z: \\rwdc01\downloads
   /user:contoso\Administrator

5. When the program prompts you for a password, type **Pa$$w0rd** and press Enter.

6. Run the ImageX.exe program to capture an image of the computer's C: drive and save it to the server, as shown in Figure 4-4, using the following syntax (where NYC-CLa is the actual name of your workstation):

   e:\imagex.exe /capture /d: z:\NYC-CLa.wim "NYC-CLa" /verify

This ImageX.exe syntax assumes that D: is the drive on which Windows 7 is installed and E: is the Windows PE boot device. If the drive assignments on your workstation are different, adjust the drive letters as needed or ask your instructor for assistance.

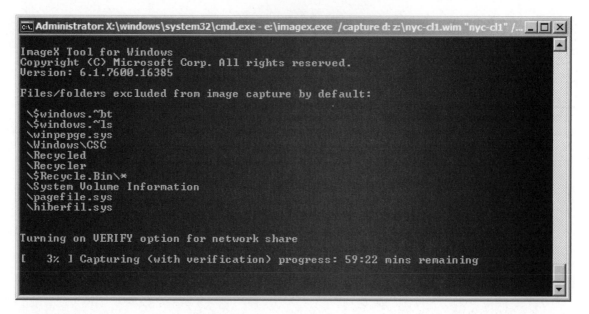

Figure 4-4
Capturing an image using ImageX.exe

7. When the image capture process is completed (which can take some time), use the following command to display the image files on the server drive:

```
dir z:\*.wim
```

Question 4	What is the exact size of the image file you created, in bytes?

8. Restart the computer and remove the Windows PE boot disk from the drive.

9. Complete the Set Up Windows screens that appear and rejoin the workstation to the Contoso domain, as you did in Exercises 3.1 and 3.2.

 NOTE *The workstation will require you to supply a user name on the Set Up Windows screen that is different from the one you supplied the first time. Instead of **student**, use the name **student2**.*

10. Log off of the computer.

LAB CHALLENGE 4.1: CREATING A CAPTURE IMAGE

Completion time	15 minutes

To complete this challenge, you must use the classroom server console to create a capture image that you can use to create an image of a workstation using Windows Deployment Services. Write out the exact steps you must perform to create the capture image, and then take a screen shot of the Image Properties sheet for the capture image you have created. You do not have to actually use the capture image on a workstation, just create it on the server console.

NOTE

In a classroom lab environment with only one server, students will have to take turns on the server console working on this challenge. In this case, be sure to include the name of your workstation in your capture image file name to differentiate it from those belonging to other students.

LAB 5
DEPLOYING A CAPTURED IMAGE

This lab contains the following exercises and activities:

Exercise 5.1	Using DISM.exe
Exercise 5.2	Installing Microsoft Deployment Toolkit 2010
Exercise 5.3	Creating a Deployment Share
Exercise 5.4	Creating a Task Sequence
Exercise 5.5	Deploying an Image
Lab Challenge 5.1	Configuring a Multicast Deployment

BEFORE YOU BEGIN

The lab environment consists of student workstations connected to a local area network, along with a server that functions as the domain controller for a domain called contoso.com. The computers required for this lab are listed in Table 5-1.

Table 5-1
Computers required for Lab 5

Computer	*Operating System*	*Computer Name*
Server	Windows Server 2008 R2	RWDC01
Workstation 1	Windows 7 Enterprise	NYC-CLa
Workstation 2	Windows 7 Enterprise	NYC-CLb

> *In a classroom lab environment, there will be one classroom server and the students will have workstations named using consecutive numbers in place of the a and b variables. In a virtual lab environment, each student will have three virtual machines, named RWDC01, NYC-CL1, and NYC-CL2.*

In addition to the computers, you will also require the software listed in Table 5-2 to complete Lab 5.

Table 5-2
Software required for Lab 5

Software	Location
Microsoft Deployment Toolkit 2010 installation files	\\rwdc01\downloads\MicrosoftDeploymentToolkit2010_x64.msi
Windows 7 Automated Installation Kit	Installed in Lab 4
Windows 7 Enterprise installation files	\\rwdc01\downloads\win7ent
Image file captured in Lab 3	\\rwdc01\downloads\NYC-CLa.wim
Lab 5 student worksheet	Lab05_worksheet.rtf (provided by instructor)

> *This manual assumes the use of the 64-bit version of Windows 7 Enterprise. If you are working in a classroom lab that uses the 32-bit version, you must use the 32-bit version of all additional software as well.*

Working with Lab Worksheets

Each lab in this manual requires that you answer questions, shoot screen shots, and perform other activities that you will document in a worksheet named for the lab, such as Lab05_worksheet.rtf. Your instructor will provide you with access to the worksheets. It is recommended that you use a USB flash drive to store your worksheets, so that you can submit them to your instructor for review. As you perform the exercises in each lab, open the appropriate worksheet file using WordPad, fill in the required information, and save the file to your flash drive.

SCENARIO

As a continuation of your Windows 7 workstation deployment project planning, you have been given the task of installing Microsoft Deployment Toolkit 2010 and using it to deploy an image file to a workstation.

After completing this lab, you will be able to:

- Use DISM.exe to modify an image file

- Install MDT 2010

- Create a deployment share and a task sequence

- Deploy an image to a workstation

Estimated lab time: 70 minutes

Exercise 5.1	Using DISM.exe
Overview	In Exercise 5.1, you use the DISM.exe utility supplied with Windows 7 AIK to mount and modify an image file.
Completion time	15 minutes

NOTE	*In a classroom lab environment, each student should have installed Windows 7 AIK on his or her own workstation during Lab 3, and should perform this exercise individually.*

1. Log on to NYC-CLa using the **contoso\Administrator** user account and the password **Pa$$w0rd**.

2. Click Start, and then click All Programs > Accessories. Right click the Command Prompt icon and, from the context menu, select *Run as administrator*. A User Account Control message box appears.

3. Click Yes to continue. A Command Prompt window appears.

4. Create a new directory on your workstation using the following two commands:

```
cd\
md mount
```

5. Use the DISM.exe program to mount your captured image with the following command:

```
dism /mount-wim /wimfile:\\rwdc01\downloads\NYC-
CLa.wim /index:1 /mountdir:c:\mount
```

6. Take a screen shot of the Command Prompt window displaying the completed DISM.exe command by pressing Alt+Prt Scr and then paste it into your Lab05_worksheet file in the page provided by pressing Ctrl+V.

7. Use the following command to list the status of the Windows 7 features in the mounted image and save the information to a text file:

```
dism /image:c:\mount /get-features > features.txt
```

8. Use the following command to display the text file you just created in Notepad, as shown in Figure 5-1:

```
notepad features.txt
```

```
test - Notepad

File   Edit   Format   View   Help

Deployment Image Servicing and Management tool
Version: 6.1.7600.16385

Image Version: 6.1.7600.16385

Features listing for package : Microsoft-Windows-Foundation-Package~31bf

Feature Name : OEMHelpCustomization
State : Disabled

Feature Name : CorporationHelpCustomization
State : Disabled

Feature Name : SimpleTCP
State : Disabled

Feature Name : SNMP
State : Disabled

Feature Name : WMISnmpProvider
State : Disabled
```

Figure 5-1
The features.txt file you created, opened in Notepad.

Question 1	What is the current status of the Solitaire feature in the mounted image?

9. In the Command Prompt window, use the following command to enable Solitaire in the mounted image:

```
dism /image:c:\mount /enable-feature
/featurename:Solitaire
```

Question 2	Why does the command fail to enable the Solitaire feature?

Question 3	*What commands must you use to enable Solitaire?*

10. Issue the necessary commands to enable Solitaire and take a screen shot of the Command Prompt window showing their successful completion by pressing Alt+Prt Scr and then paste it into your Lab05_worksheet file in the page provided by pressing Ctrl+V.

11. Use the following command to commit your changes to the image and dismount it:

```
dism /unmount-wim /mountdir:c:\mount /commit
```

Question 4	*Although DISM.exe is a standard executable program, its command line parameters bear a resemblance to what Windows administrative environment?*

12. Type **exit** and press Enter. The Command Prompt window closes.

13. Leave the computer logged on for the next exercise.

Exercise 5.2	Installing Microsoft Deployment Toolkit 2010
Overview	In Exercise 5.2, you install MDT 2010 so that you can use its tools to perform a practice Windows 7 workstation deployment.
Completion time	5 minutes

NOTE	*If you have not already installed the Windows 7 Automated Installation Kit on your workstation, as described in Exercise 4.1, do so before you proceed with this exercise.*

1. Click Start. In the *Search programs and files* box, type **\\rwdc01\downloads\MicrosoftDeploymentToolkit2010_x64.msi** and press Enter. The Microsoft Deployment Toolkit 2010 Setup Wizard appears.

2. Click Next to bypass the *Welcome* page. The *End-User License Agreement* page appears.

3. Select the *I accept the terms of the license agreement* option and click Next. The *Custom Setup* page appears.

4. Click Next to accept the default settings. The *Ready to Install* page appears.

5. Click Install. The wizard installs the toolkit and the *Completing the Microsoft Deployment Toolkit 2010 Setup Wizard* page appears.

6. Click Finish.

7. Leave the computer logged on for the next exercise.

Exercise 5.3	Creating a Deployment Share
Overview	In Exercise 5.3, you use the tools provided with MDT 2010 to create a deployment share.
Completion time	10 minutes

1. Click Start. Then click All Programs > Microsoft Deployment Toolkit > Deployment Workbench. The Deployment Workbench console appears, as shown in Figure 5-2.

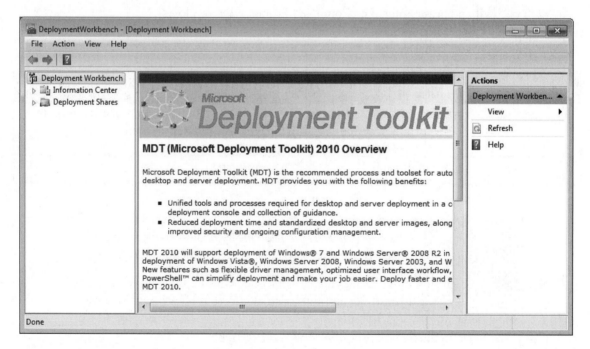

Figure 5-2
The Deployment Workbench

2. Right click the Deployment Shares folder and, from the context menu, select New Deployment Share. The New Deployment Share Wizard appears.

3. Click Next to accept the default share location. The *Share* page appears.

4. Click Next to accept the default share name. The *Descriptive Name* page appears.

5. Click Next to accept the default descriptive name. The *Allow Image Capture* page appears.

6. Click Next to accept the default setting. The *Allow Admin Password* page appears.

7. Select the Ask user to set the local Administrator Password check box and click Next. The *Allow Product Key* page appears.

8. Click Next to accept the default setting. The *Summary* page appears.

9. Click Next. The wizard creates the deployment share and the *Confirmation* page appears.

10. Click Finish.

11. Expand the Deployment Shares folder and the folder for the deployment share you just created.

12. Select the Operating Systems folder, then right click it and, from the context menu, select Import Operating System. The Import Operating System Wizard appears, displaying the *OS Type* page.

13. Leave the *Full set of source files* option selected and click Next. The *Source* page appears.

14. In the *Source directory* text box, type **\\rwdc01\downloads\win7ent** and click Next. The *Destination* page appears.

15. Click Next to accept the default directory name. The *Summary* page appears.

16. Click Next. The wizard imports the image file and the *Confirmation* page appears.

17. Click Finish. The wizard closes and the image appears in the Operating Systems folder.

18. Take a screen shot of the Deployment Workbench console showing the imported image by pressing Alt+Prt Scr and then paste it into your Lab05_worksheet file in the page provided by pressing Ctrl+V.

19. Leave the Deployment Workbench console open for the next exercise.

Exercise 5.4	Creating a Task Sequence
Overview	In Exercise 5.4, you use Deployment Workbench to create a task sequence that deploys Windows 7.
Completion time	15 minutes

1. In the Deployment Workbench console, select the Task Sequences folder, right click it and, from the context menu, select New Task Sequence. The New Task Sequence Wizard appears, displaying the *General Settings* page, as shown in Figure 5-3.

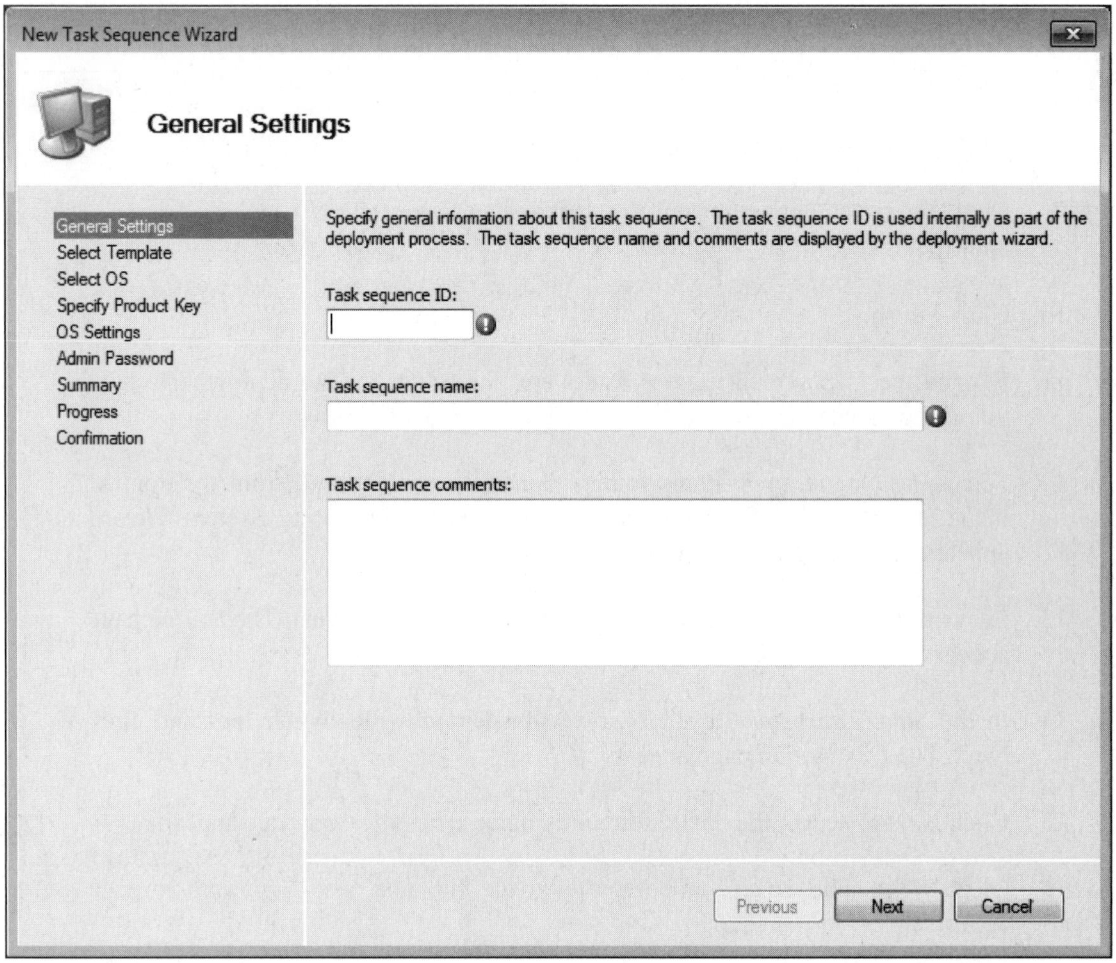

Figure 5-3
The New Task Sequence Wizard

2. In the *Task sequence ID* text box, type **1**.

3. In the *Task sequence name* text box, type **Windows 7 Enterprise Deployment** and click Next. The *Select Template* page appears.

4. Leave the Standard Client Task Sequence template selected and click Next. The *Select OS* page appears.

5. Select the Windows 7 image you imported and click Next. The *Specify Product Key* page appears.

6. Click Next to accept the default option. The *OS Settings* page appears.

7. In the Full Name text box, type your name, and in the Organization text box, type the name of your school. Then click Next. The *Administrator Password* page appears.

8. In the Administrator Password and Please confirm Administrator Password text boxes, type **Pa$$w0rd** and click Next. The *Summary* page appears.

9. Click Next. The wizard creates the task sequence and the *Confirmation* page appears.

10. Click Finish. The wizard closes and the task sequence appears in the console.

11. Right click the task sequence and, from the context menu, select Properties. The Windows 7 Enterprise Deployment Properties sheet for the task sequence appears.

12. Click the Task Sequence tab, and browse to the Preinstall > New Computer only > Format and Partition Disk node, as shown in Figure 5-4.

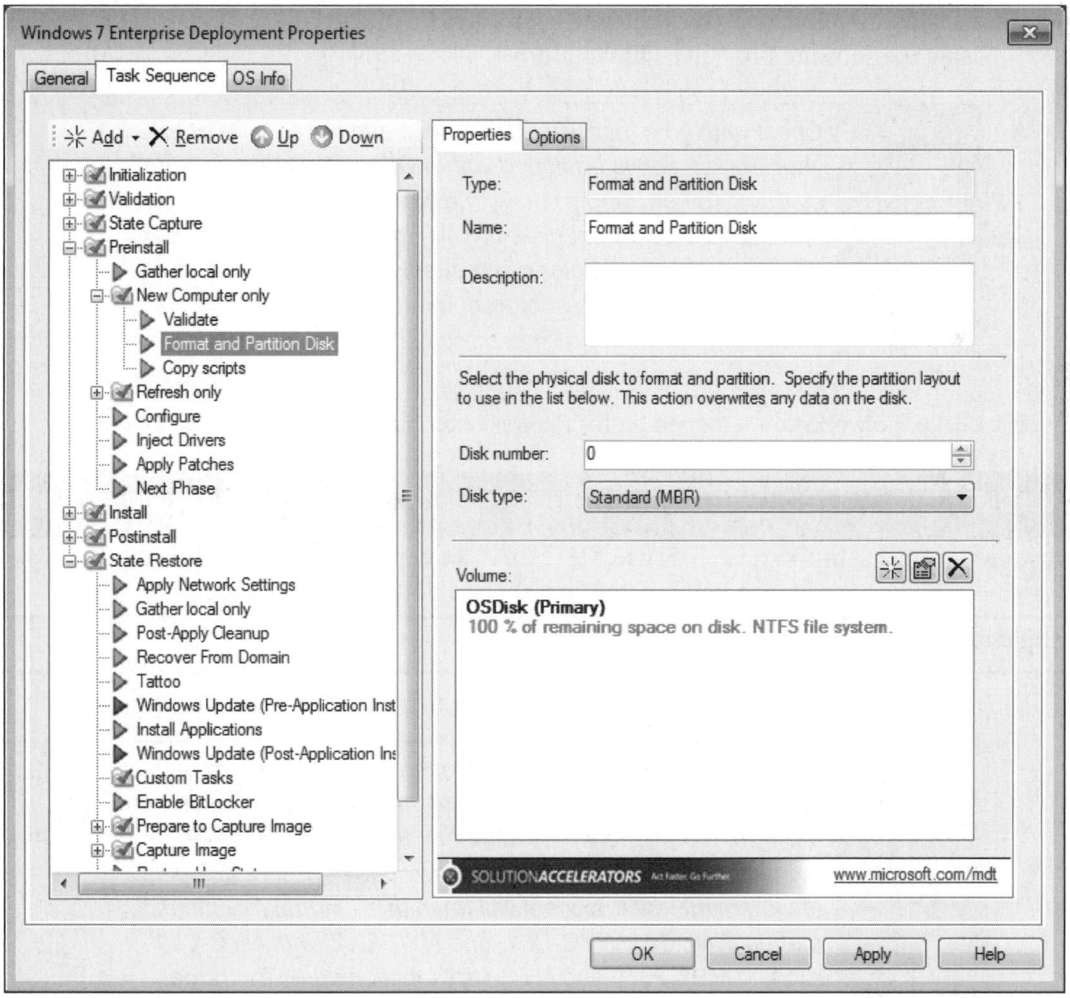

Figure 5-4
The Format and Partition Disk node

13. Select the OSDisk (Primary) volume and click the Properties button. The Partition Properties dialog box appears.

14. Change the Size (%) value to 66 and click OK.

15. Click OK to close the Windows 7 Enterprise Deployment Properties sheet.

16. Right click the deployment share and, from the context menu, select Update Deployment Share. The Update Deployment Share Wizard appears, displaying the *Options* page.

17. Click Next to accept the default option. The *Summary* page appears.

18. Click Next. The wizard updates the deployment share and creates deployment image files. The *Confirmation* page appears.

19. Click Finish.

20. Burn the LiteTouchPE_x64.iso image created by Deployment Workbench, located in the C:\DeploymentShare\Boot folder, to a CD-ROM or DVD-ROM, using the software provided with your drive.

 *Check with your instructor before you attempt to burn a disk. If your workstation is equipped with a CD or DVD burner, your instructor might supply you with a blank disk and a procedure for burning your own boot disk. If your workstation is not properly equipped, your instructor might supply you with a boot disk or instructions on how to boot from the network.*

21. Leave the workstation logged on for the next exercise.

Exercise 5.5	Deploying an Image
Overview	In Exercise 5.5, use MDT 2010 to deploy an image file using the task sequence you created in Exercise 5.4.
Completion time	20 minutes

In a classroom lab environment, students should perform this exercise with a partner so that they have one workstation running MDT 2010 and one workstation functioning as the target computer to which they will deploy Windows 7. In a virtual lab environment, each student will have three virtual machines, named RWDC01, NYC-CL1, and NYC-CL2, with NYC-CL1 running MDT 2010 and NYC-CL2 functioning as the target computer.

1. Start the NYC-CLb computer using the LiteTouchPE_x64 boot disk you created in Exercise 5.4. The system boots to the Welcome Windows Deployment window, as shown in Figure 5-5.

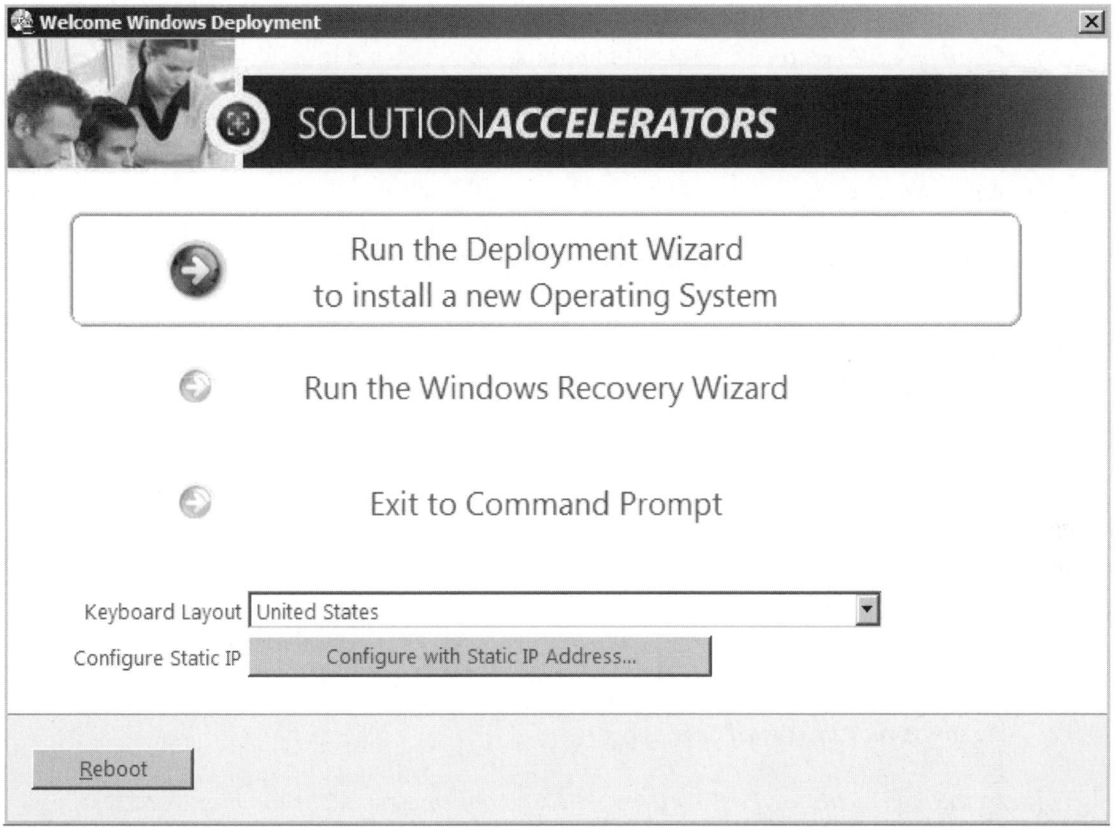

Figure 5-5
The Welcome Windows Deployment window

Question 5	Which computer is hosting the Deployment Wizard?

2. Click *Run the Deployment Wizard to install a new Operating System.* The *Specify credentials for connecting to network shares* page appears.

3. Enter the required credentials as follows and click OK:

    - User name: **Administrator**
    - Password: **Pa$$w0rd**
    - Domain: **contoso**

    The *Select a task sequence to execute on this computer* page appears.

4. Take a screen shot of the *Select a task sequence to execute on this computer* page by pressing Alt+Prt Scr and then paste it into your Lab05_worksheet file in the page provided by pressing Ctrl+V.

5. Select the Windows 7 Enterprise Deployment task sequence and click Next. The *Configure the computer name* page appears.

6. In the Computer name text box, type **NYC-CLb** where b is the number assigned to the computer and click Next. The *Join the computer to a domain or workgroup* page appears.

7. Select the *Join a domain* option and, in the Domain text box, type **contoso.com** and click Next. The *Specify whether to restore user data* page appears.

Question 6	If you elected to restore user data, what program would the target computer use to perform the restoration?

8. Click Next to accept the default option. The *Language and other preferences* page appears.

9. Click Next to accept the default options. The *Set the Time Zone* page appears.

10. Select the appropriate time zone for your location and click Next. The *Administrator Password* page appears.

11. In the *Administrator Password* and *Please confirm Administrator Password* text boxes, type **Pa$$w0rd** and click Next. The *Specify the BitLocker configuration* page appears.

12. Click Next to accept the default option. The *Ready to Begin* page appears.

13. Click the Details button.

14. Take a screen shot of the *Ready to begin* page by pressing Alt+Prt Scr and then paste it into your Lab05_worksheet file in the page provided by pressing Ctrl+V.

15. Click Begin. The Windows 7 deployment proceeds, the computer restarts, and the *Operating system deployment completed successfully* page appears.

16. Click Finish. The *Set Network Location* page appears.

17. Click Work network. A *Windows could not set the network settings* page appears.

18. Click Close.

19. Log off of the computer.

LAB CHALLENGE 5.1: CONFIGURING A MULTICAST DEPLOYMENT

Completion time	5 minutes

To complete this challenge, you must use the classroom server console to create a multicast transmission in Windows Deployment Services that triggers when there are five workstations requesting deployment. Write out the exact steps you must perform to create the multicast transmission, and then take a screen shot of the Windows Deployment Services console, showing the multicast transmission you have created. You do not have to actually perform a multicast deployment, just create it on the server console.

 *In a classroom lab environment with only one server, students will have to take turns on the server console working on this challenge. In this case, be sure to include the name of your workstation in your capture image filename to differentiate it from those belonging to other students.*

LAB 6
WORKING WITH DISKS

This lab contains the following exercises and activities:

BEFORE YOU BEGIN

The lab environment consists of student workstations connected to a local area network, along with a server that functions as the domain controller for a domain called contoso.com. The computers required for this lab are listed in Table 6-1.

Table 6-1
Computers required for Lab 6

Computer	Operating System	Computer Name
Server	Windows Server 2008 R2	RWDC01
Workstation 1	Windows 7 Enterprise	NYC-CLa

NOTE	*In a classroom lab environment, there will be one classroom server and the students will have workstations named using consecutive numbers in place of the a and b variables. In a virtual lab environment, each student will have three virtual machines, named RWDC01, NYC-CL1, and NYC-CL2.*

In addition to the computers, you will also require the software listed in Table 6-2 to complete Lab 6.

Table 6-2
Software required for Lab 6

Software	Location
Windows 7 Enterprise installation files	\\rwdc01\downloads\win7ent
Lab 6 student worksheet	Lab06_worksheet.rtf (provided by instructor)

Working with Lab Worksheets

Each lab in this manual requires that you answer questions, shoot screen shots, and perform other activities that you will document in a worksheet named for the lab, such as Lab06_worksheet.rtf. Your instructor will provide you with access to the worksheets. It is recommended that you use a USB flash drive to store your worksheets, so that you can submit them to your instructor for review. As you perform the exercises in each lab, open the appropriate worksheet file using WordPad, fill in the required information, and save the file to your flash drive.

SCENARIO

You are a desktop technician working at the help desk in a medium-sized organization. One morning, a user named Alice calls and complains that she created an important document file for her boss yesterday, saved it to her hard drive, and now cannot find it. Alice goes on to explain that this sort of thing happens to her all the time: she creates files and saves them, and when she tries to open them again, she must spend half an hour looking for them. Sometimes she finds the file she needs and sometimes she doesn't, which forces her to create it all over again.

When you examine Alice's hard disk, you find document files strewn about the drive everywhere, some intermixed with application files and others stored in the root of the drive. You decide to show Alice the basics of file management, starting with how to create a new partition for her data and thereby keep it separate from her application and operating system files.

Thanks to your discussion, Alice now sees the advantage of storing her data files on a partition separate from the operating system and application files.

After completing this lab, you will be able to:

- Create a basic primary partition

- Create an extended partition and logical drives

- Convert a basic disk to a dynamic disk

- Create dynamic disk volumes

- Extend and shrink dynamic volumes

- Mount a volume in an NTFS folder

Estimated lab time: 75 minutes

Exercise 6.1	Creating a Basic Disk Partition
Overview	In Exercise 6.1, you create a new basic partition for Alice where she can store her data.
Completion time	10 minutes

1. Turn on the NYC-CLa workstation and log on using the **contoso\Administrator** account and the password **Pa$$w0rd**.

2. Click Start, and then click Control Panel. The Control Panel window appears.

3. Click System And Security > Administrative Tools. The Administrative Tools window appears.

4. Double click Computer Management. The Computer Management console appears.

5. Select Disk Management. The Disk Management snap-in appears, as shown in Figure 6-1.

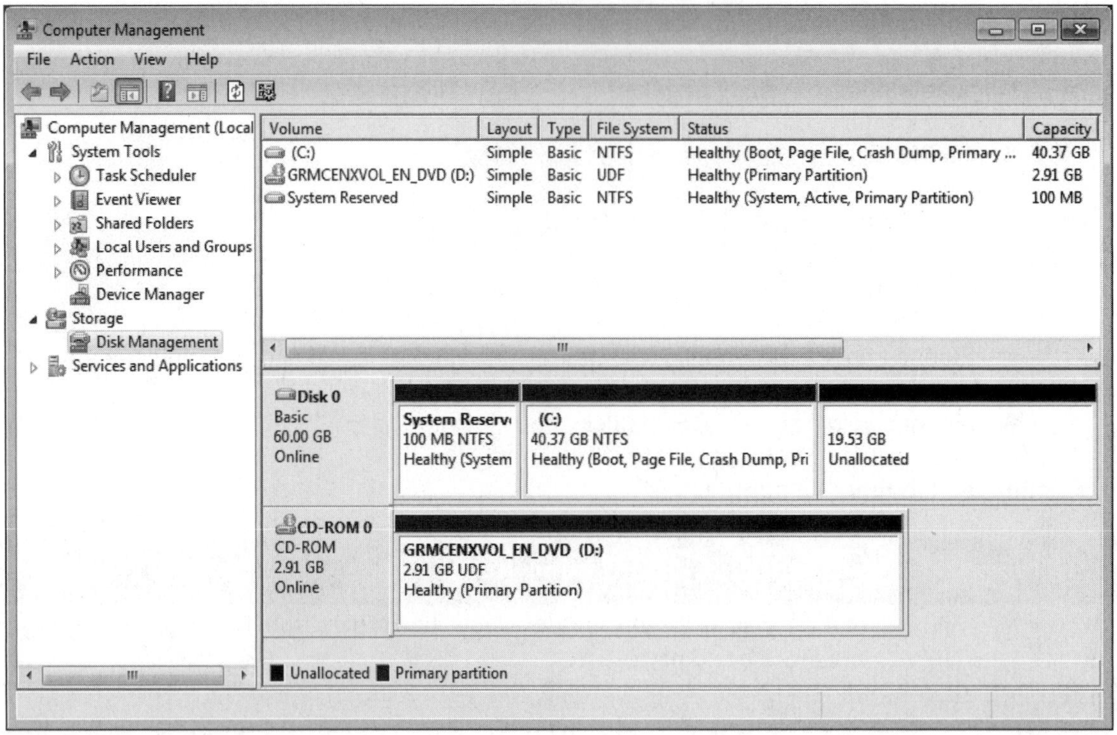

Figure 6-1
The Disk Management snap-in

6. Based on the information in the Disk Management snap-in, fill out the information in Table 6-3 on your lab worksheet.

Table 6-3
Disk information

	Disk 0
Disk type (basic or dynamic)	basic
Total disk size	60 GD
Number and type of partitions	1 NTFS
Amount of unallocated space	~~60000ub~~ 19.53 GB

> **NOTE**
>
> *If there is not at least 1GB of unallocated space available on your workstation, see your instructor before you continue.*

7. In the graphical display in the bottom view pane, select the unallocated area of Disk 0. Right click the unallocated area and, from the context menu, select New Simple Volume. The New Simple Volume Wizard appears.

8. Click Next to bypass the *Welcome* page. The *Specify Volume Size* page appears.

9. In the Simple volume size in MB text box, type **20000** and click Next. The *Assign Drive Letter or Path* page appears.

10. Leave the *Assign the following drive letter* option selected, and then choose drive letter X from the drop-down list and click Next. The *Format Partition* page appears.

11. Leave the *Format this volume with the following settings* option selected, and configure the next three parameters as follows:

    - File system: FAT32
    - Allocation unit size: Default
    - Volume label: Alice1

12. Leave the Perform a quick format check box selected and click Next. The *Completing the New Simple Volume Wizard* page appears.

13. Click Finish. The new volume appears in the Disk Management snap-in and an Autoplay window appears, displaying various options for the use of the new X: volume.

14. Click Open folder to view files. An Explorer window appears, displaying the X: drive.

15. Leave the computer logged on for the next exercise.

Exercise 6.2	Extending a Basic Disk Partition
Overview	A few days later, you receive another call at the help desk from Alice. She has been diligently moving her data files to the special partition you created for her, but she has now run out of disk space. The partition was not big enough! To address the problem, you decide to extend the Alice1 partition, using some of the unallocated space left on the disk. For this task, you intend to use the Diskpart.exe command line utility.
Completion time	15 minutes

1. In the Explorer window you opened in Exercise 6.1, expand the Network container and the RWDC01 server object. Then select the downloads folder.

2. Copy the entire win7ent folder from RWDC01\downloads to the X: drive you created in Exercise 6.1.

3. A message box appears, stating that there is insufficient space on the X: drive to complete the copy.

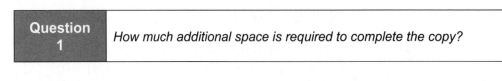

4.   Take a screen shot of the message box by pressing Alt+Prt Scr and then paste it into your Lab06_worksheet file in the page provided by pressing Ctrl+V.

5.   Click Cancel.

6.   Consult the Disk Management snap-in, and fill out Table 6-4 with the amount of unallocated space left on the drive in gigabytes and megabytes.

Table 6-4
Unallocated space remaining

	Disk 0
Unallocated space left (in gigabytes)	
Unallocated space left (in megabytes)	

7.   Click Start. Then click All Programs > Accessories > Command Prompt. A Command Prompt window appears.

8.   In the Command Prompt window, type **diskpart** and press Enter. A DISKPART> prompt appears.

9.   Type **select disk 0** and press Enter. The program responds, indicating that disk 0 is now the selected disk.

10. Type **list partition** and press Enter. A list of the partitions on disk 0 appears, as shown in Figure 6-2.

```
Administrator: Command Prompt - diskpart                                    _  □  ✕

C:\Users\Administrator>diskpart

Microsoft DiskPart version 6.1.7600
Copyright (C) 1999-2008 Microsoft Corporation.
On computer: NYC-CL1

DISKPART> select disk 0

Disk 0 is now the selected disk.

DISKPART> list partition

  Partition ###  Type              Size     Offset
  -------------  ----------------  -------  -------
  Partition 1    Primary           100 MB   1024 KB
  Partition 2    Primary            40 GB    101 MB
  Partition 3    Primary            19 GB     40 GB

DISKPART>
```

Figure 6-2
A list of partitions displayed by Diskpart.exe

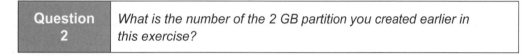

Question 2	What is the number of the 2 GB partition you created earlier in this exercise?

11. Type **select partition #,** where # is the number of the 2 GB partition, and press Enter. The program responds, saying that partition # is now the selected partition.

12. Type **extend size=xxxx**, where xxxx is the amount of unallocated space left on the drive, in megabytes, from Table 6-4, and press Enter.

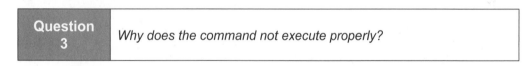

Question 3	Why does the command not execute properly?

13. Type **exit** and press Enter. The DISKPART program terminates, returning you to the standard command prompt.

14. At the command prompt, type **convert x: /fs:ntfs /v /x** and press Enter. The system prompts you for the volume label of the X: drive.

15. Type **Alice1** and press Enter. The system successfully completes the conversion of the volume from FAT32 to NTFS.

16. Run the Diskpart.exe program again and repeat steps 9 through 12.

Question 4	What is the result?

17. Type **exit** and press Enter to terminate the Diskpart program.

18. Close the Command Prompt window.

19. In the Explorer window, try again to copy the RWDC01\downloads\win7ent folder to the X: drive.

Question 5	What is the result?

20. Leave the computer logged on for the next exercise.

Exercise 6.3	Creating Additional Partitions
Overview	Alice is thrilled at the idea of storing her data files in separate partitions, and now she wants you to create more partitions on her drive. However, you used all of the available space to create her Alice1 partition. Therefore, you must shrink the Alice1 partition to create room for the additional partitions that she wants. In Exercise 6.3, you create additional partitions.
Completion time	10 minutes

1. In the Disk Management snap-in, right click the Alice1 volume you created on Disk 0 and, from the context menu, select Shrink Volume. The Shrink X: dialog box appears, as shown in Figure 6-3.

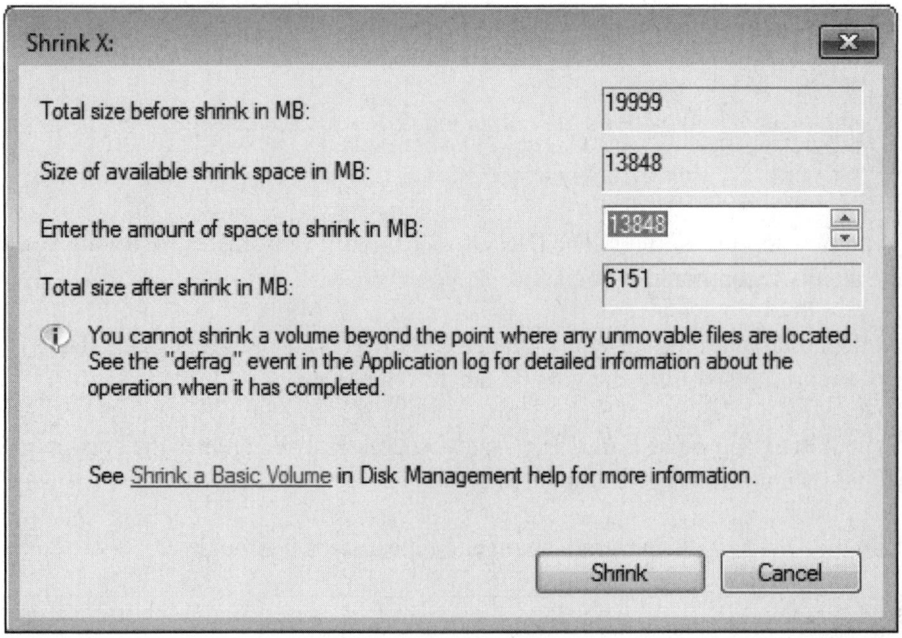

Figure 6-3
The Shrink X: dialog box

Question 6	How much available shrink space can be found in the volume? *20384*

2. In the *Enter the amount of space to shrink in MB* spin box, type the amount of available shrink space minus 2000 MB (2 GB).

3. Click Shrink. The amount of space you entered appears as unallocated space in the Disk Management snap-in.

4. Right click the unallocated space and select New Simple Volume. The New Simple Volume Wizard appears.

5. Use the wizard to create a new **2000 MB** partition using the drive letter Y:, the NTFS file system, and the volume name **Alice2**.

Question 7	How is the resulting volume different from the one you created in Exercise 6.1? Explain why. *iT is smaller disc size.*

Question 8	Why doesn't the extended partition that you created appear in the Disk Management snap-in's volume list in the top view pane? *alice 2(Y) does appear*

Question 9	What would happen if you created another simple volume out of the free space left on the disk? *The space vould get smaller.*

6. Take a screen shot of the Disk Management snap-in that shows the volumes you created by pressing Ctrl+Prt Scr, and then paste the resulting image into the Lab06_worksheet file in the page provided by pressing Ctrl+V.

7. Leave the computer logged on for the next exercise.

Exercise 6.4	Mounting a Volume
Overview	Alice calls the help desk yet again to tell you that she needs still more space on her Alice1 partition, but is unable to expand it. In Exercise 6.4, you provide her with additional space by creating a volume and mounting it in a folder on the Alice1 volume.
Completion time	15 minutes

1. In the Disk Management snap-in, right click the Alice1 volume you created in Exercise 6.1 and try to extend it by 2000 MB.

2. Now right click the Alice2 volume you created in Exercise 6.3 and try to extend it by 2000 MB.

Question 10	Why were you able to extend the Alice2 volume, but not the Alice1 volume? *Cannot extend either*

3. In Windows Explorer, create a new folder on the computer's X: drive called **Alice3**.

4. In the Disk Management snap-in, right click the remaining *Free space* element on Disk 0 and, from the context menu, select New Simple Volume.

5. In the New Simple Volume Wizard, specify a volume size of 2000 MB.

6. On the *Assign Drive Letter or Path* page, select the *Mount in the following empty NTFS folder* option. In the text box, type **x:\Alice3** and click Next.

7. On the *Format Partition* page, select the NTFS file system and assign the volume the label **Alice3**. Then click Next.

8. Click Finish to create the volume.

9. In Windows Explorer, right click the X: drive, and open its Properties sheet.

Question 11	According to Windows Explorer, what is the capacity of the X: drive?

Question 12	Does the capacity shown for the X: drive in Windows Explorer reflect the addition of the mounted volume?

10. Click OK to close the Alice1 (X:) Properties sheet.

11. Right click the Alice3 folder icon and, from the context menu, select Properties. The Alice3 Properties sheet appears.

Question 13	Why doesn't the Properties sheet display the capacity of the Alice3 volume?

12. Click the Properties button. The Properties sheet for the disk volume appears.

Question 14	What is the capacity of Alice3?

13. Click OK twice to close the two Properties sheets.

14. Leave the computer logged on for the next exercise.

Exercise 6.5	Working with Dynamic Disks
Overview	Alice currently has five partitions on her basic disk: three primary partitions and one extended partition with two logical drives. She has found it difficult to manage her files with so many partitions, so she wants to consolidate the disk into just three volumes—her original two plus one large data volume—that will be part of a striped volume. Unfortunately, the second hard disk drive for Alice's computer is back-ordered, so you cannot create the stripe set yet. However, in Exercise 6.5 you are going to prepare for the upgrade by converting the basic disk to a dynamic disk and consolidating the partitions. Alice has already copied all of her files from the Alice2 and Alice3 volumes to Alice1.
Completion time	10 minutes

1. In the Disk Management snap-in, in the graphical display, right click the Disk 0 box and, from the context menu, select Convert to Dynamic Disk. The Convert to Dynamic Disk dialog box appears.

2. Leave the default Disk 0 check box selected and click OK. The Disks to Convert dialog box appears, as shown in Figure 6-4.

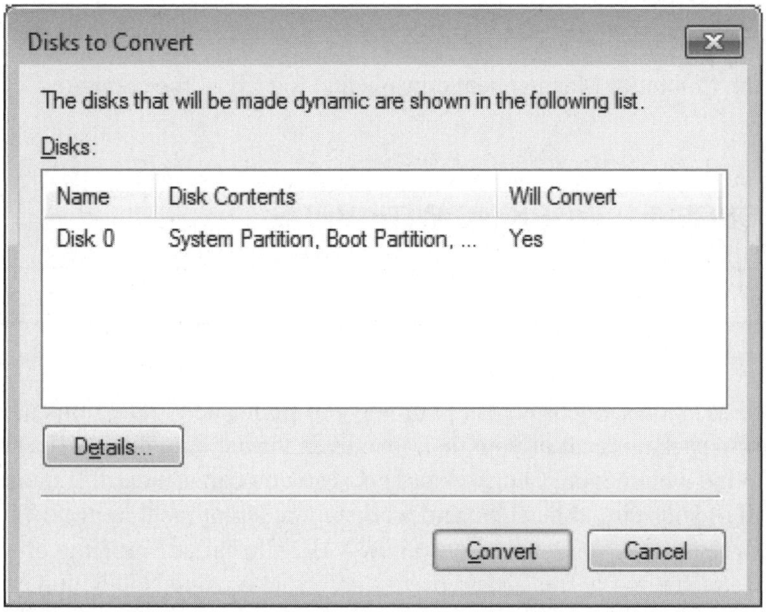

Figure 6-4
The Disks to Convert dialog box

3. Click Convert. A Disk Management message box appears, warning you that after you convert the disk to a dynamic disk, you will not be able to start installed operating systems from any volume other than the current boot volume.

4. Click Yes to continue. The snap-in performs the disk conversion.

Question 15	What has happened to the primary partitions and logical drives that you created earlier in this lab?

Question 16	After you converted the basic disk to a dynamic disk, how many partitions can be found on the disk?

5. Take a screen shot of the Disk Management snap-in that shows the dynamic volumes you created by pressing Ctrl+Prt Scr, and then paste the resulting image into the Lab06_worksheet file in the page provided by pressing Ctrl+V.

6. Right click the Alice3 volume and, from the context menu, select Delete Volume. A Delete Simple Volume dialog box appears.

7. Click Yes to confirm that you want to delete the volume. The Alice3 volume reverts to unallocated space.

8. Delete the Alice2 volume using the same procedure.

9. Right click the Alice1 volume and, from the context menu, select Extend Volume. The Extend Volume Wizard appears.

10. Using the wizard, extend the volume using all of the remaining unallocated space on the disk.

11. Close the Computer Management console and log off of the computer.

LAB CHALLENGE 6.1: WORKING WITH VHDS

Completion time	15 minutes

As part of the Windows 7 deployment planning you performed in previous labs, you are considering packaging all of your disk images as virtual hard disk (VHD) files, rather than Windows Imaging (wim) files. This is so you can standardize on one format for all of your virtual machine and workstation deployment images. To complete this challenge, you must create a new VHD file called Win7img on your workstation, attach it to the file system partition, format it using NTFS, and copy the entire contents of the \\RWDC01\downloads\win7ent folder to it. Write out the steps you performed to complete these tasks and take a screen shot of the Disk Management snap-in, showing the VHD.

LAB 7
CONFIGURING NETWORK CONNECTIONS

This lab contains the following exercises and activities:

Exercise 7.1   Using the Network and Sharing Center

Exercise 7.2   Enabling Network Map

Exercise 7.3   Manually Configuring TCP/IP

Exercise 7.4   Testing Network Connections

Lab Challenge 7.1   Using Nslookup.exe

BEFORE YOU BEGIN

The lab environment consists of student workstations connected to a local area network, along with a server that functions as the domain controller for a domain called contoso.com. The computers required for this lab are listed in Table 7-1.

Table 7-1
Computers required for Lab 7

Computer	Operating System	Computer Name
Server	Windows Server 2008 R2	RWDC01
Workstation 1	Windows 7 Enterprise	NYC-CLa
Workstation 2	Windows 7 Enterprise	NYC-CLb

> NOTE
>
> *In a classroom lab environment, there will be one classroom server and the students will have workstations named using consecutive numbers in place of the a and b variables. In a virtual lab environment, each student will have three virtual machines, named RWDC01, NYC-CL1, and NYC-CL2.*

In addition to the computers, you will also require the software listed in Table 7-2 to complete Lab 7.

Table 7-2
Software required for Lab 7

Software	Location
Lab 7 student worksheet	Lab07_worksheet.rtf (provided by instructor)

Working with Lab Worksheets

Each lab in this manual requires that you answer questions, shoot screen shots, and perform other activities that you will document in a worksheet named for the lab, such as Lab07_worksheet.rtf. Your instructor will provide you with access to the worksheets. It is recommended that you use a USB flash drive to store your worksheets, so that you can submit them to your instructor for review. As you perform the exercises in each lab, open the appropriate worksheet file using WordPad, fill in the required information, and save the file to your flash drive.

SCENARIO

You are a Windows 7 technical specialist for Contoso, Ltd., a company with workstations in a variety of different environments. The IT director wants to create a permanent software testing lab where engineers can run updates and new applications prior to deploying them on the network. The lab will consist of a network that can function in complete isolation from the company's production network. You have been assigned the task of building the lab network using Windows 7 computers borrowed from the production network.

After completing this lab, you will be able to:

■ Use the Windows 7 Network and Sharing Center

■ Use Network Map

■ Manually configure the Windows 7 TCP/IP client

■ Test network connections with Ping.exe

Estimated lab time: 55 minutes

Exercise 7.1	Using the Network and Sharing Center
Overview	On a Windows 7 computer, the Network and Sharing Center provides access to most of the operating system's networking tools and configuration parameters. In Exercise 7.1, you examine the current Sharing and Discovery settings on one of the computers that will become part of the lab network.
Completion time	10 minutes

1. Turn on the NYC-CLa workstation and log on using the **contoso\Administrator** account and the password **Pa$$w0rd**.

2. Click Start and then click Control Panel. The Control Panel window appears.

3. Click Network and Internet > Network and Sharing Center. The Network and Sharing Center control panel appears, as shown in Figure 7-1.

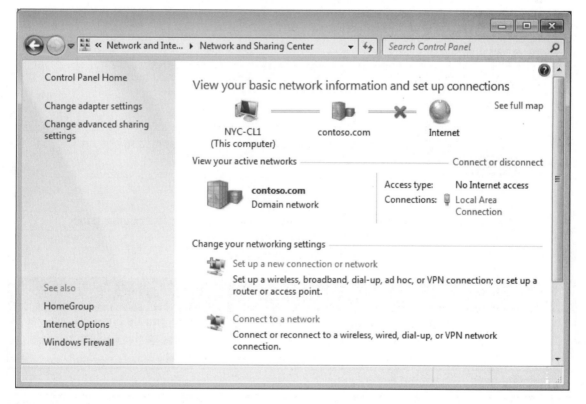

Figure 7-1
The Network and Sharing Center

4. Click *See full map*. The network map fails to appear.

Question 1	Why did the network map fail to appear?

5. Click the back arrow to return to the Network and Sharing Center control panel.

6. Click *Change advanced sharing settings*. The *Change sharing options for different network profiles* window appears.

7. In Table 7-3, note the current state of the advanced Sharing and Discovery settings.

Table 7-3
Advanced Sharing and Discovery Settings

Setting	Value
Network discovery	On
File and printer sharing	On
Public folder sharing	Off
Media streaming	Off
File sharing connections	128-bit

Question 2	Could the current state of the advanced sharing settings be the reason why the network map fails to appear?

8. Click the back arrow to return to the Network and Sharing Center control panel.

9. Leave the computer logged on for the next exercise.

Exercise 7.2	Enabling Network Map
Overview	In Exercise 7.2, you use local Group Policy to enable Network Map to display a diagram of the network, so you can plan the software deployments for the lab network at a later time.
Completion time	10 minutes

1. Click Start, and in the *Search programs and files* box, type **mmc** and press Enter. A blank Microsoft Management Console window appears.

2. Click File > Add/Remove Snap-in. The Add or Remove Snap-ins dialog box appears, as shown in Figure 7-2.

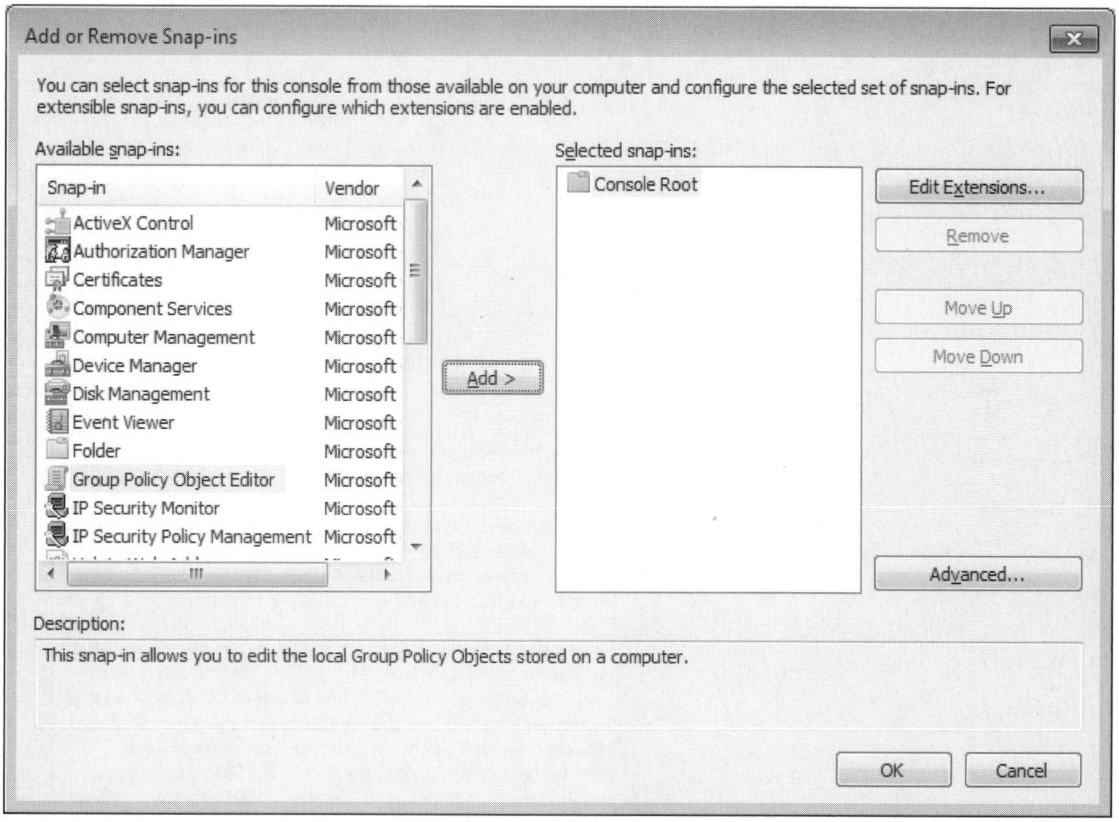

Figure 7-2
The Add or Remove Snap-ins dialog box

3. In the Available snap-ins list, select Group Policy Object Editor and click Add. The Select Group Policy Object Wizard appears.

4. Click Finish to accept the default Local Computer Group Policy Object.

5. Click OK to close the Add or Remove Snap-ins dialog box. The Local Computer Policy node appears in the MMC console.

6. Browse to the Computer Configuration\Administrative Templates\Network\Link-Layer Topology Discovery folder.

7. Double click the *Turn on Mapper I/O (LLTDIO) driver* policy. The Turn on Mapper I/O (LLTDIO) driver dialog box appears, as shown in Figure 7-3.

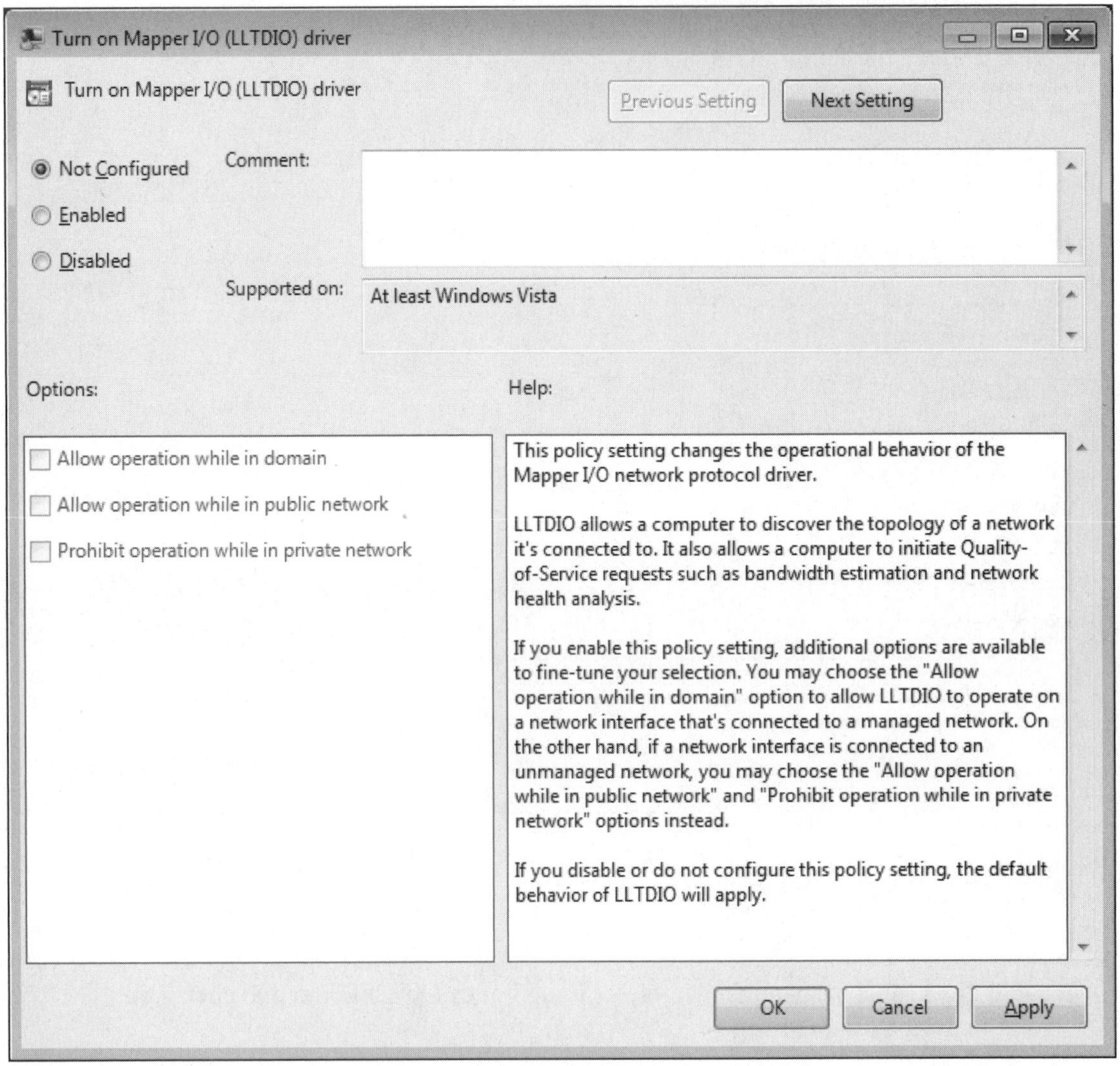

Figure 7-3
The Turn on Mapper I/O (LLTDIO) driver dialog box

8. Click Enabled and then select the *Allow operation while in domain* check box. Then click OK.

9. Double click the *Turn on Responder (RSPNDR) driver* policy. The Turn on Responder (RSPNDR) driver dialog box appears.

10. Click Enabled and then select the *Allow operation while in domain* check box. Then click OK.

11. Switch back to the Network and Sharing Center control panel and click *See full map* again. The Network Map window appears, displaying a diagram of the network.

NOTE	*If you are working in a classroom lab, you might have to wait for other students to configure their workstations before the Network Map appears, In a virtual lab, you will have to repeat this entire exercise on your NYC-CLb workstation before the Network Map can appear.*

12. Take a screen shot of the Network Map window by pressing Alt+Prt Scr, and then paste the resulting image into the Lab07_worksheet file in the page provided by pressing Ctrl+V.

Question 3	*Why does the RWDC01 computer not appear on the Network Map display?*

13. Leave the computer logged on for the next exercise.

Exercise 7.3	Manually Configuring TCP/IP
Overview	Because the lab network you are constructing for Contoso, Ltd. must be isolated from the production network, you do not want the lab computers to obtain their TCP/IP settings from the DHCP servers on the production network. Therefore, in Exercise 7.3 you manually configure the TCP/IP client to use static IP addresses.
Completion time	15 minutes

1. Click Start. Then click All Programs > Accessories > Command Prompt. A Command Prompt window appears.

2. In the Command Prompt window, type **ipconfig /all** and press Enter.

3. Using the information in the Ipconfig.exe display, note your workstation's current TCP/IP configuration settings in Table 7-4.

Table 7-4

TCP/IP Setting		Value
IPv4 Address	192. 168. 98. 134	
Subnet Mask	255 . 255. 255, 0	
Default Gateway	192 . 168. 98. 2	
DNS Servers	192. 168. 98. 2	

Question 4	*How did the computer obtain these settings? How can you determine this?*

4. In the Command Prompt window, type **ipconfig /release** and press Enter.

Question 5	*What is the result of this command?*

5. In the Network and Sharing Center control panel, click *Change adapter settings*. The Network Connections window appears.

6. Right click the Local Area Connection icon and, from the context menu, select Properties. The Local Area Connection Properties sheet appears.

7. Select Internet Protocol Version 4 (TCP/IPv4) from the components list and click Properties. The Internet Protocol Version 4 (TCP/IPv4) Properties sheet appears, as shown in Figure 7-4.

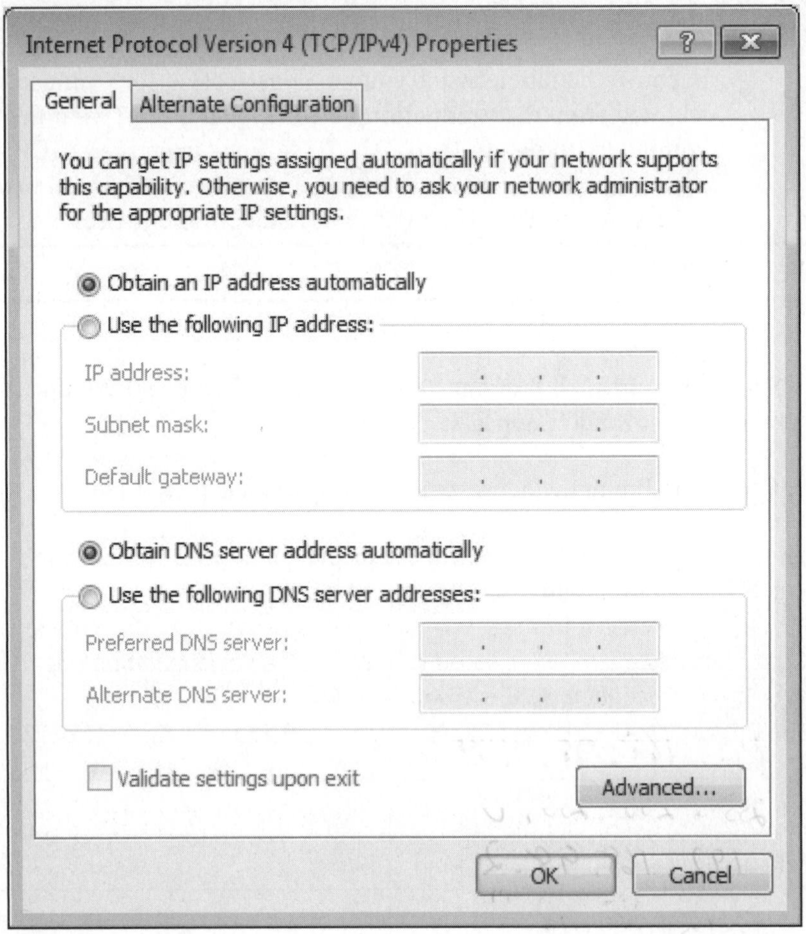

Figure 7-4
The Internet Protocol Version 4 (TCP/IPv4) Properties sheet

8. Select *Use the following IP address.*

9. In the IP address text box, type the IPv4 Address value from Table 7-4, changing the address from 10.10.0.x to 10.10.1.x.

10. In the Subnet mask text box, type the Subnet Mask value from Table 7-4.

11. In the Preferred DNS server text box, type the DNS Server value from Table 7-4.

Question 6	Which of the parameters in the Internet Protocol Version 4 (TCP/IPv4) Properties sheet would you have to omit for your computer to be unable to resolve a computer name into its IP address?

12. Take a screen shot of the Internet Protocol Version 4 (TCP/IPv4) Properties sheet by pressing Alt+Prt Scr, and then paste the resulting image into the Lab07_worksheet file in the page provided by pressing Ctrl+V.

13. Click OK to close the Internet Protocol Version 4 (TCP/IPv4) Properties sheet.

14. Click OK to close the Local Area Connection Properties sheet.

15. In the Command Prompt window, run the **ipconfig /all** command again.

Question 7	How does the Ipconfig display differ from the first time you ran the ipconfig /all command? *it auto configed*

16. Leave the computer logged on for the next exercise.

NOTE	If you are working in a virtual lab environment, you must repeat this entire exercise on your NYC-CLb workstation before proceeding to Exercise 7.4.

Exercise 7.4	Testing Network Connections
Overview	After manually configuring the Windows 7 TCP/IP client, you must test it by trying to connect to the other computers on the network. In Exercise 7.4, you use the Ping utility to test the computer's communications capabilities.
Completion time	10 minutes

1.   In the Command Prompt window, type **ping 127.0.0.1** and press Enter.

Question 8	What is the result?

Question 9	What does this result prove about the computer's network connectivity?

Question 10	What would be the result if you unplugged your computer's network cable before executing the ping 127.0.0.1 command?

2.   In the Command Prompt window, type **ping rwdc01** and press Enter.

Question 11	What is the result of the ping test, and what does it prove?

Question 12	What is the IP address of RWDC01?

Question 13	How was the computer able to resolve the name RWDC01 into its IP address?

3.   Using the IP address of another computer on the network, test your connectivity to it using the command **ping *ipaddress.***

NOTE	If you are working in a classroom lab, ask your lab partner for the IP address of his or her workstation. If you are working in a virtual lab environment, use the IP address of your NYC-CLb workstation.

Question 14	What was the result of the test, and what does this result prove?

4.   From the other workstation, ping your computer using the IP address you assigned to it in Exercise 7.3.

Question 15	*What was the result of the test, and what does this result prove?*

Question 16	*Was it necessary to perform this last test? Why or why not?*

5.   Log off of the computer.

LAB CHALLENGE 7.1: USING NSLOOKUP.EXE

Completion time	10 minutes

Nslookup.exe is a command line utility that enables administrators to test specific functionalities of the Domain Name System (DNS). To complete this challenge, you must list the proper Nslookup commands that will perform the following tasks:

- Display the NSLOOKUP prompt.
- Set the default domain name to contoso.com.
- Set RWDC01 to function as the default DNS server.
- Resolve the name of your workstation.

LAB 8
WORKING WITH SHARES

This lab contains the following exercises and activities:

Exercise 8.1   Setting Up a Workstation

Exercise 8.2   Sharing a Folder

Exercise 8.3   Using the Shared Folders Snap-In

Exercise 8.4   Configuring NTFS Permissions

Lab Challenge 8.1 Compressing Files and Folders

BEFORE YOU BEGIN

The lab environment consists of student workstations connected to a local area network, along with a server that functions as the domain controller for a domain called contoso.com. The computers required for this lab are listed in Table 8-1.

Table 8-1
Computers required for Lab 8

Computer	Operating System	Computer Name
Server	Windows Server 2008 R2	RWDC01
Workstation 1	Windows 7 Enterprise	NYC-CLa
Workstation 2	Windows 7 Enterprise	NYC-CLb

In a classroom lab environment, there will be one classroom server and the students will have workstations named using consecutive numbers in place of the a and b variables. In a virtual lab environment, each student will have three virtual machines, named RWDC01, NYC-CL1, and NYC-CL2.

In addition to the computers, you will also require the software listed in Table 8-2 to complete Lab 8.

Table 8-2
Software required for Lab 8

Software	Location
Windows 7 Enterprise installation files	\\RWDC01\downloads\win7ent
Lab 8 student worksheet	Lab08_worksheet.rtf (provided by instructor)

Working with Lab Worksheets

Each lab in this manual requires that you answer questions, shoot screen shots, and perform other activities that you will document in a worksheet named for the lab, such as Lab08_worksheet.rtf. Your instructor will provide you with access to the worksheets. It is recommended that you use a USB flash drive to store your worksheets, so that you can submit them to your instructor for review. As you perform the exercises in each lab, open the appropriate worksheet file using WordPad, fill in the required information, and save the file to your flash drive.

SCENARIO

You are a Windows 7 technical specialist for Contoso, Ltd., a company with workstations in a variety of different environments. You are currently assigned to the desktop support help desk and, as a result, you are faced with a number of problems concerning file sharing and access control.

After completing this lab, you will be able to:

- Create and control access to shares

- Use the Shared Folders snap-in

- Modify NTFS permissions

Estimated lab time: 45 minutes

Exercise 8.1   Setting Up a Workstation

Overview	Complete Exercise 8.1 to prepare your workstation for the subsequent exercises in this lab.
Completion time	5 minutes

1. Turn on the NYC-CLa workstation and log on using the **contoso\Administrator** account and the password **Pa$$w0rd**.

2. Click Start and then click Control Panel. The Control Panel window appears.

3. Click System and Security > Administrative Tools. Then double click Computer Management. The Computer Management console appears.

4. Expand the Local Users and Groups node and select the Users folder.

5. Double click the Guest user account. The Guest Properties sheet appears.

6. Clear the Account is disabled check box and click OK.

7. Right click the Guest account and, from the context menu, select Set Password. A Set Password for Guest message box appears, warning you of possible issues when you reset the password.

8. Click Proceed. The Set Password for Guest dialog box appears.

9. In the *New password* and *Confirm password* text boxes, type **Pa$$w0rd** and click OK.

10. A message box appears, informing you that the password has been set.

> **NOTE**   *Make sure that the Student account appears in the Users folder. If it does not appear, you must create one, using the password Pa$$w0rd.*

11. Close the Computer Management console.

12. Click Start, and in the Search programs and files box, type **\\RWDC01\downloads\win7ent** and press Enter. An Explorer window appears, displaying the contents of the win7ent folder.

13. Copy the entire support folder from the win7ent folder on server RWDC01 to the C: drive on your workstation.

14. Leave the computer logged on for the next exercise.

Exercise 8.2	Sharing a Folder
Overview	Luz, a user with a Windows 7 workstation, has files on her local drive that she must share with other users on the network. However, these files must not be fully accessible to everyone. As the technical specialist responding to Luz's request, you decide to create a standard share on the computer and use share permissions to control access to the files.
Completion time	10 minutes

1. In Windows Explorer, right click the support folder you created on your workstation's C: drive in Exercise 8.1 and, from the context menu, select Properties. The support Properties sheet appears.

2. Click the Sharing tab, and then click Advanced Sharing. The Advanced Sharing dialog box appears, as shown in Figure 8-1.

Figure 8-1
The Advanced Sharing dialog box

3. Select the *Share this folder* check box. The **support** default value appears in the *Share name* text box.

4. Click Permissions. The Permissions for support dialog box appears.

5. Select the Everyone special identity and clear all of the check boxes in the Allow column.

6. Click Add. The Select Users, Computers, Service Accounts, or Groups dialog box appears.

7. In the Enter the object names to select box, type **Domain Admins** and click OK. The Domain Admins group appears in the *Group or user names* list in the Permissions for support dialog box.

8. Select the Domain Admins group and then, in the Permissions for Domain Admins box, select the Full Control check box in the Allow column, which causes the Change check box to be selected as well.

9. Using the same technique, add the Domain Users group to the *Group or user names* list, and assign it the Allow Change and Allow Read permissions.

10. Add the Guest user account to the *Group or user names* list, and assign it the Allow Read permission only.

11. Take a screen shot of the Permissions for support dialog box by pressing Alt+Prt Scr, and then paste the resulting image into the Lab08_worksheet file in the page provided by pressing Ctrl+V.

12. Click OK to close the Permissions for support dialog box.

13. Click OK to close the Advanced Sharing dialog box.

14. Click Close to close the Support Properties sheet.

15. Log off of the workstation.

16. Using another workstation on the network, log on using the **contoso\Guest** account with the password **Pa$$w0rd**.

> NOTE
>
> *If you are working in a classroom lab environment, you can switch workstations with your lab partner. In a virtual lab environment, you can use your NYC-CL2 workstation.*

17. Click Start. Then, in the *Search programs and files* box, type **nyc-cla\support**, where a is the number of the workstation where you created the share. A Network Error window appears, as shown in Figure 8-2, informing you that you do not have permission to access \\nyc-cla\support.

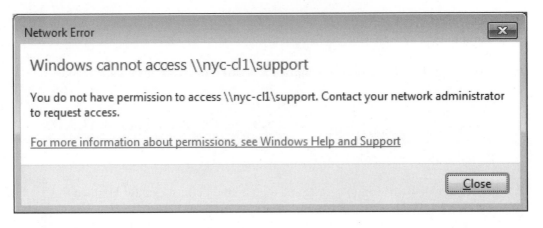

Figure 8-2
The Network Error window

Question 1	*Why are you unable to access the share using the Guest account, despite having granted the user the Allow Read permission?*

Question 2	*Would the Guest user be able to access the share if you granted it the Allow Full Control share permission, rather than the Allow Read permission?*

18. Log off of the workstation, and then log on again using the **contoso\Administrator** account with the password **Pa$$w0rd**.

19. Try again to open the **\\nyc-cla\support** share from the *Search programs and files* box. An Explorer window appears, displaying the contents of the support folder.

20. Leave the workstation logged on for the next exercise.

Exercise 8.3	Using the Shared Folders Snap-In
Overview	Luz wants to be able to tell who is accessing her shares at any particular time, so in Exercise 8.3 you demonstrate to her the functionality of the Shared Folders snap-in.
Completion time	10 minutes

1. Back at your NYC-CLa workstation, log on using the **contoso\Administrator** account and the password **Pa$$w0rd**.

2. Click Start. Then, right click Computer and, from the context menu, select Manage. The Computer Management console appears.

3. Expand the Shared Folders node and select the Sessions folder.

Question 3	How many currently open sessions are there on the workstation? Which computers and which users are accessing the workstation's shares?

4. Right click the Sessions folder and, from the context menu, select Disconnect All Sessions. A Shared folders message box appears, asking you to confirm that you want to close all sessions.

5. Click Yes. The open sessions in the folder disappear.

6. Select the Shares folder, as shown in Figure 8-3.

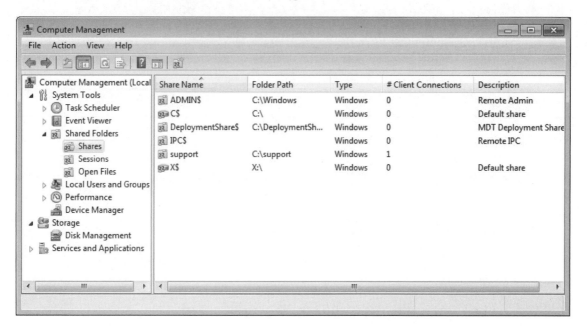

Figure 8-3
The Shares folder in the Shared Folders snap-in

Question 4	How many shares are there on the computer that are visible to network users? How can you tell?

7. Right click the Shares folder and, from the context menu, select New Share. The Create a Shared Folder wizard appears.

8. Click Next to bypass the *Welcome* page. The *Folder Path* page appears.

9. In the Folder path text box, type **C:\Users** and click Next. The *Name, Description, and Settings* page appears.

10. Click Next to accept the default settings. The *Shared Folder Permissions* page appears.

11. Select the *Administrators have full access; other users have read-only access* option and click Finish. The *Sharing Was Successful* page appears.

12. Click Finish. The new Users share appears in the Shares folder.

13. Take a screen shot of the console by pressing Alt+Prt Scr, and then paste the resulting image into the Lab08_worksheet file in the page provided by pressing Ctrl+V.

14. Close the Computer Management console.

Exercise 8.4	Configuring NTFS Permissions
Overview	To enable network users to access the files in Luz's shared folders, they must have the appropriate NTFS permissions. In Exercise 8.4, you configure the permissions to enable the guest user to access the shared folder.
Completion time	10 minutes

1. In Windows Explorer, right click the support folder you created on your workstation's C: drive in Exercise 8.1 and, from the context menu, select Properties. The support Properties sheet appears.

2. Click the Security tab. Then click Edit. The Permissions for support dialog box appears, as shown in Figure 8-4.

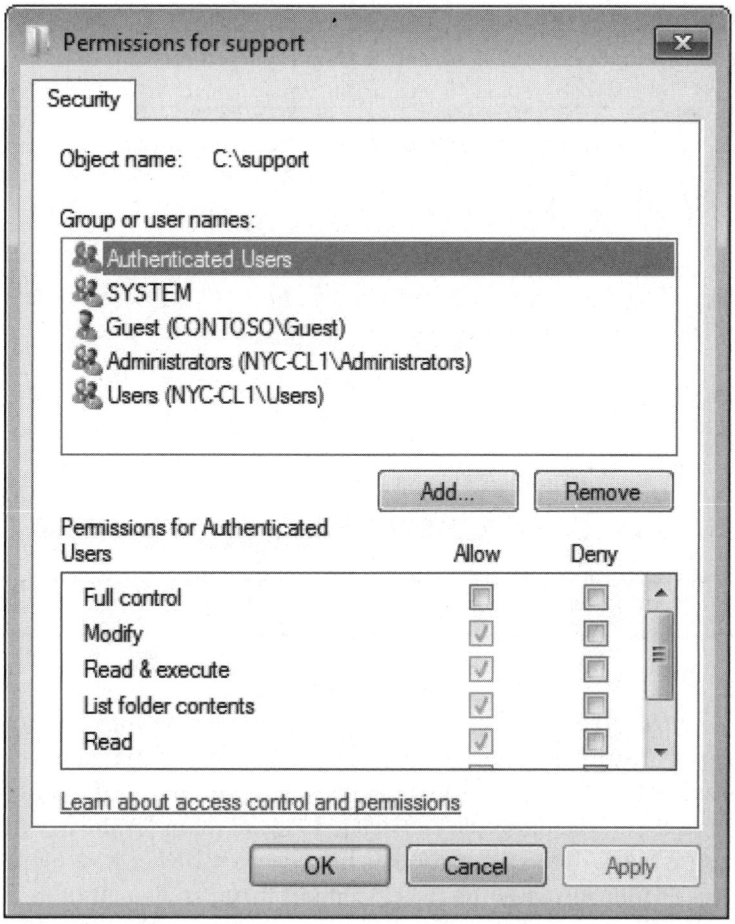

Figure 8-4
The Permissions for support dialog box

3. Click Add. The Select Users, Computers, Service Accounts, or Groups dialog box appears.

4. In the Enter the object names to select box, type **Guest** and click OK. The Guest user appears in the *Group or user names* list in the Permissions for support dialog box.

5. Select the Guest user and then, in the Permissions for Guest box, select the Modify check box in the Allow column, which causes the Write check box also to be selected.

6. Click OK to close the Permissions for support dialog box.

7. Click Close to close the support Properties sheet.

8. Log off of the workstation.

9. Using another workstation on the network once again, log on using the **contoso\Guest** account with the password **Pa$$w0rd**.

10. Click Start. Then, in the *Search programs and files* box, type **nyc-cla\support**, where a is the number of the workstation where you created the share.

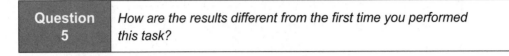

Question 5	*How are the results different from the first time you performed this task?*

11. Click Start. Then, in the *Search programs and files* box, type **nyc-cla\support**, where a is the number of the workstation where you created the share.

12. Log off of the workstation.

LAB CHALLENGE 8.1: COMPRESSING FILES AND FOLDERS

Completion time	10 minutes

A week later, Luz calls the help desk and tells you that she must copy a number of large files to her shared folder, but an error has appeared on her computer stating that she does not have enough disk space. Luz claims that she needs all of the files on her hard disk and that there is nothing she can delete to make room for the new files. You decide to compress some of the files on Luz's drive to provide her with more space. To complete this challenge, configure the C:\support folder so that all of its current files, and all of the files that Luz places there, are compressed. Write out the instructions you performed to complete the task.

LAB 9
WORKING WITH PRINTERS

This lab contains the following exercises and activities:

Exercise 9.1   Installing a Printer

Exercise 9.2   Sharing a Printer

Exercise 9.3   Controlling Access to a Printer

Exercise 9.4   Creating an Additional Logical Printer

Lab Challenge 9.1   Creating a Printer Pool

BEFORE YOU BEGIN

The lab environment consists of student workstations connected to a local area network, along with a server that functions as the domain controller for a domain called contoso.com. The computers required for this lab are listed in Table 9-1.

Table 9-1
Computers required for Lab 9

Computer	Operating System	Computer Name
Server	Windows Server 2008 R2	RWDC01
Workstation 1	Windows 7 Enterprise	NYC-CLa

In a classroom lab environment, there will be one classroom server and the students will have workstations named using consecutive numbers in place of the a and b variables. In a virtual lab environment, each student will have three virtual machines, named RWDC01, NYC-CL1, and NYC-CL2.

In addition to the computers, you will also require the software listed in Table 9-2 to complete Lab 9.

Table 9-2
Software required for Lab 9

Software	Location
Lab 9 student worksheet	Lab09_worksheet.rtf (provided by instructor)

Working with Lab Worksheets

Each lab in this manual requires that you answer questions, shoot screen shots, and perform other activities that you will document in a worksheet named for the lab, such as Lab09_worksheet.rtf. Your instructor will provide you with access to the worksheets. It is recommended that you use a USB flash drive to store your worksheets, so that you can submit them to your instructor for review. As you perform the exercises in each lab, open the appropriate worksheet file using WordPad, fill in the required information, and save the file to your flash drive.

SCENARIO

You are a Windows 7 technical specialist for Contoso, Ltd., a company with workstations in a variety of different environments. You have been assigned the task of installing and managing a number of new printers that the company has just received.

After completing this lab, you will be able to:

■ Install and share a printer

■ Install additional printer drivers

■ Configure advanced printer properties

■ Configure printer permissions

Estimated lab time: 55 minutes

Exercise 9.1   Installing a Printer

Overview	Contoso, Ltd. has just taken delivery of several new printers that the IT director purchased through an auction. He has assigned you the task of installing the printers and making them available to the users of the company network. For the first printer, you intend to connect the unit directly to an LPT port in the Windows 7 computer that will function as the print server. In Exercise 9.1, you install the driver for the printer and configure it to send print jobs to the LPT2 port.
Completion time	10 minutes

1. Turn on the NYC-CLa workstation and log on using the **contoso\Administrator** account and the password **Pa$$w0rd**.

2. Click Start, and then click Control Panel. The Control Panel window appears.

3. Click Hardware and Sound > Devices and Printers. The Devices and Printers control panel appears, as shown in Figure 9-1.

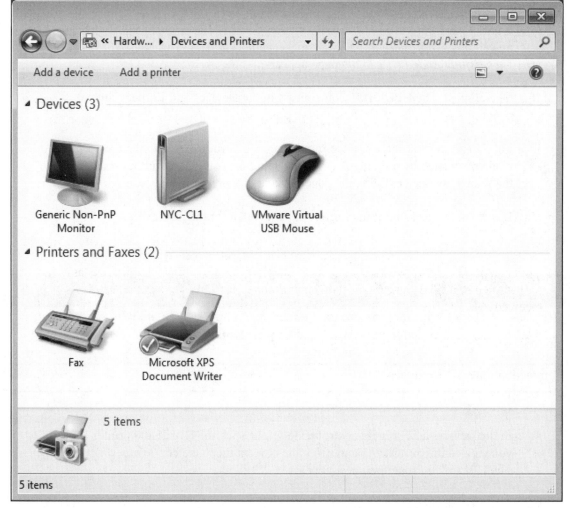

Figure 9-1
The Devices and Printers control panel

4. Click *Add a printer*. The Add Printer wizard appears, displaying the *What type of printer do you want to install?* page.

5. Click *Add a local printer*. The *Choose a printer port* page appears.

6. Leaving the *Use an existing port* option selected, select LPT2: (Printer Port) from the drop-down list and click Next. The *Install the printer driver* page appears.

Question 1	Why doesn't Windows 7 attempt to automatically detect a printer connected to the computer?

7. In the Manufacturer column, select HP. In the Printers column, select HP LaserJet 5200 Series PCL 5 and click Next. The *Type a printer name* page appears.

8. In the Printer Name text box, type **HPLJ5200** and click Next. The wizard installs the driver and the *Printer Sharing* page appears.

9. Select the *Do not share this printer* option and click Next. The *You've Successfully Added HPLJ5200* page appears.

10. Click Finish. The HPLJ5200 icon appears in the Devices and Printers control panel.

11. Take a screen shot of the Devices and Printers control panel with the new printer icon you created by pressing Alt+Prt Scr, and then paste the resulting image into the Lab09_worksheet file in the page provided by pressing Ctrl+V.

12. Leave the Devices and Printers control panel open for the next exercise.

Exercise 9.2	Sharing a Printer
Overview	With the printer installed on the computer, you are ready to make it available to network users by creating a printer share and publishing it in the Active Directory database.
Completion time	5 minutes

1. In the Devices and Printers control panel, right click the HPLJ5200 printer icon you created in Exercise 9.1 and, from the context menu, select *Printer properties*. The HPLJ5200 Properties sheet appears.

2. Click the Sharing tab, as shown in Figure 9-2.

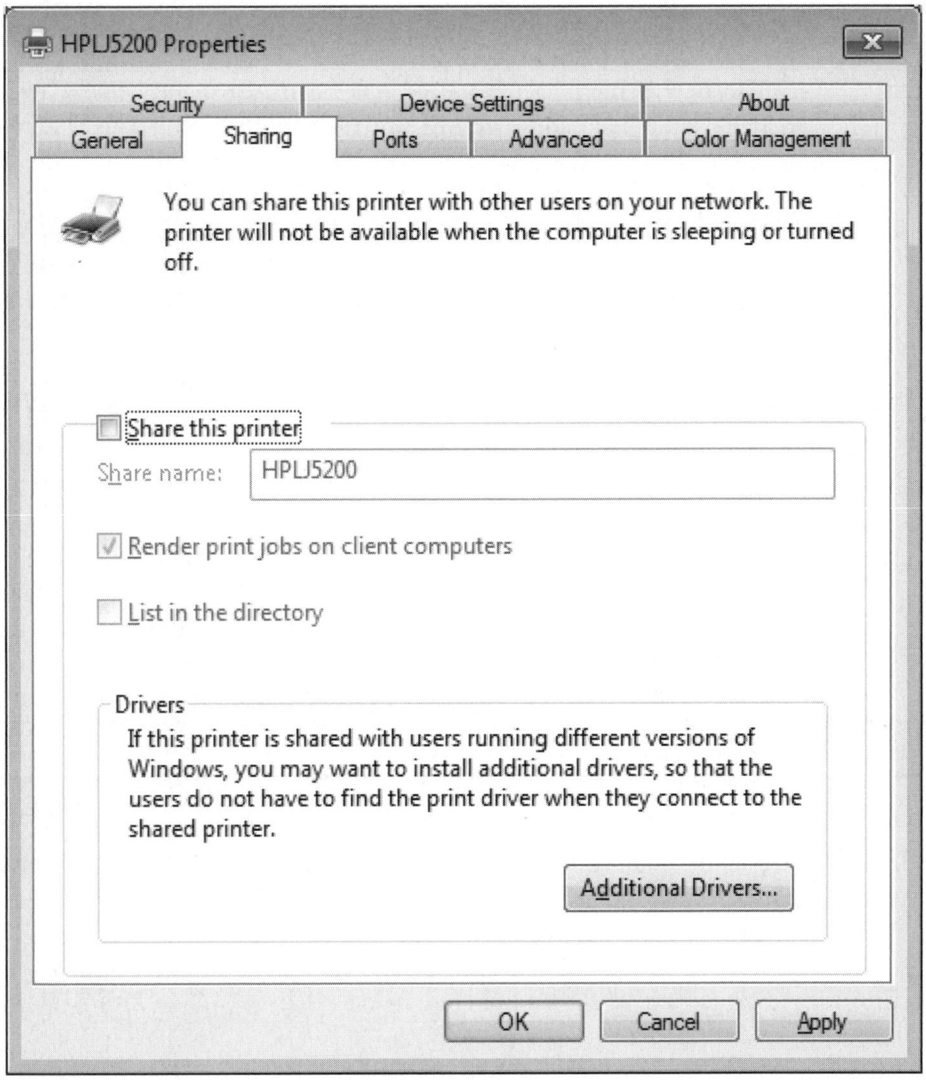

HPLJ5200 Properties   x

| Security | Device Settings | About |
| General | Sharing | Ports | Advanced | Color Management |

You can share this printer with other users on your network. The printer will not be available when the computer is sleeping or turned off.

☐ Share this printer

Share name: HPLJ5200

☑ Render print jobs on client computers

☐ List in the directory

Drivers
If this printer is shared with users running different versions of Windows, you may want to install additional drivers, so that the users do not have to find the print driver when they connect to the shared printer.

Additional Drivers...

OK   Cancel   Apply

Figure 9-2
The Sharing tab of a printer's Properties sheet

3. Select the *Share this printer* check box. Leave the *Render print jobs on client computers* check box selected, and select the *List in the directory* check box. Then click OK.

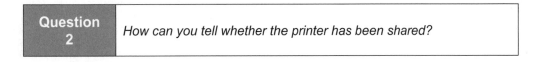

Question 2   *How can you tell whether the printer has been shared?*

4. Leave the Devices and Printers control panel open for the next exercise.

Exercise 9.3	Controlling Access to a Printer
Overview	The new printer you installed has been in use for several weeks, and there have been some administrative problems you must address. First, from reading the printer's page counter and the amount of paper consumed, it is apparent that someone is using the printer to generate an enormous amount of personal work after business hours. While it is not practical to secure the printer physically, you can restrict the hours in which it can be used. In addition, you can limit who has access to the printer by using permissions.
	Another problem is that users are sending print jobs requiring paper of various sizes to the printer, and when a specific type of paper is not available, the entire print queue is halted until someone inserts the correct paper for that particular job. There have also been several instances in which a user's computer crashed while printing a job and in which a user tried to interrupt a job as it was printing, thereby causing the queue to be stalled until the partial job was removed.
	In Exercise 9.3, you configure the advanced properties of the logical printer you created in Exercise 9.1 to create a more secure printing environment and prevent these problems from occurring.
Completion time	15 minutes

1. In the Devices and Printers control panel, right click the HPLJ5200 printer icon you created in Exercise 9.1 and, from the context menu, select *Printer properties*. The HPLJ5200 Properties sheet appears.

2. Click the Advanced tab, as shown in Figure 9-3.

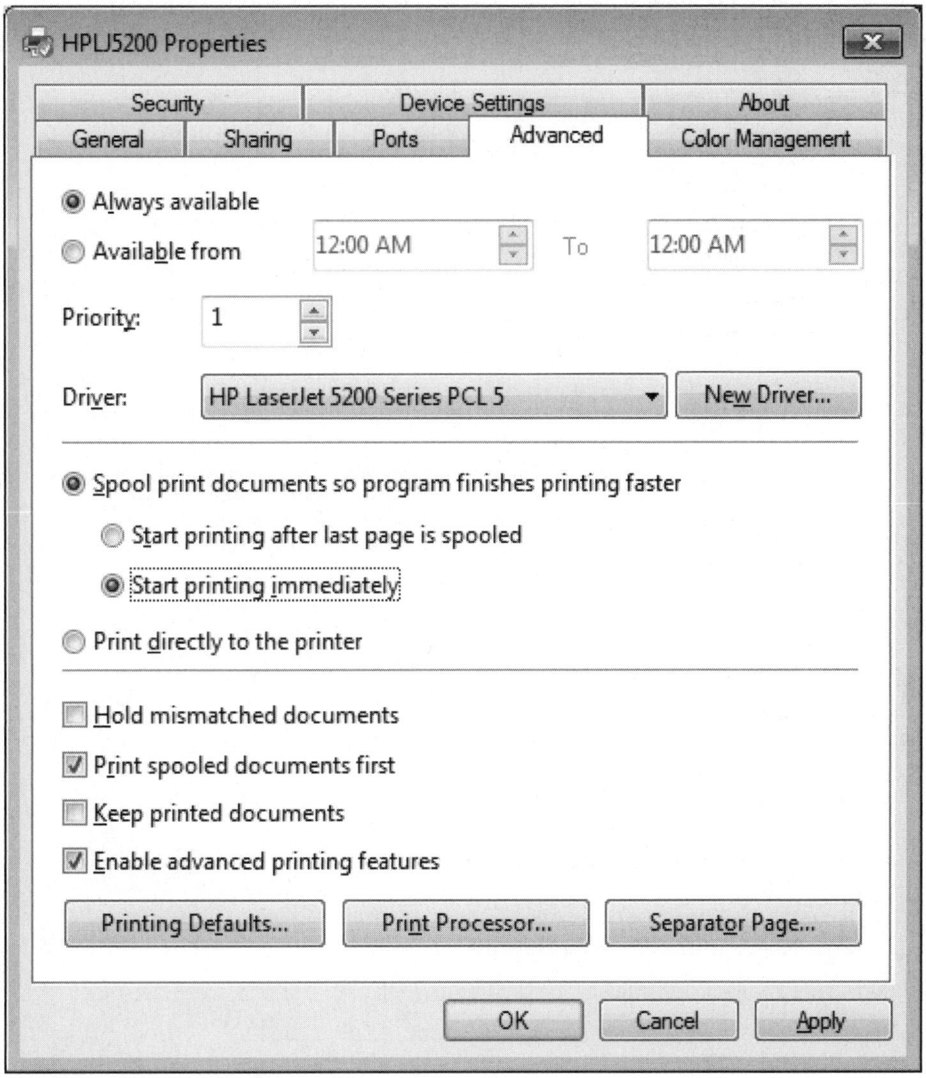

Figure 9-3
The Advanced tab of a printer's Properties sheet

3. Select the *Available from* option and, in the two spin boxes provided, set the time that the printer is available to 9:00 AM to 5:00 PM.

Question 3	Which of the problems described earlier will this setting help to prevent and how?

4. Select the *Start printing after last page is spooled* option.

5. Select the Hold mismatched documents check box.

6. Click Apply to save your changes, and then click the Security tab, as shown in Figure 9-4.

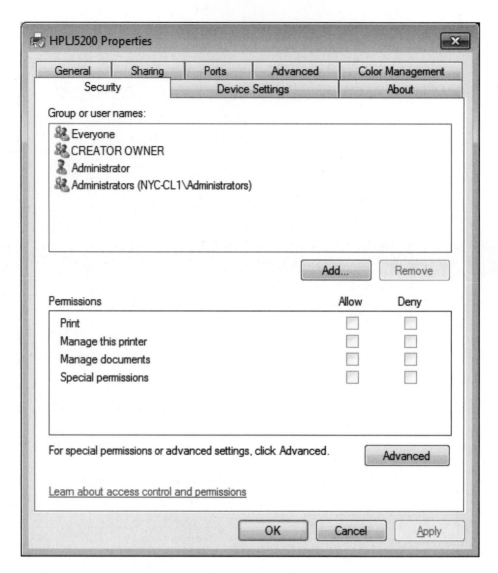

Figure 9-4
The Security tab of a printer's Properties sheet

7. In the Group or user names list, select Everyone and click Remove. The Everyone special identity is removed from the list.

8. Click Add. The Select Users, Computers, Service Accounts, or Groups dialog box appears.

9. In the Enter the object names to select box, type **Domain Users** and click OK. The Domain Users security principal appears in the Group or user names list.

10. With Domain Users highlighted, make sure that only the Print check box in the Allow column is selected.

11. Make sure that the Administrators group is listed as a security principal and is assigned the Print, Manage this printer, and Manage documents permissions in the Allow column.

12. Take a screen shot of the Security tab displaying the new permissions you created by pressing Alt+Prt Scr, and then paste the resulting image into the Lab09_worksheet file in the page provided by pressing Ctrl+V.

13. Click OK to close the Properties sheet.

14. Leave the Devices and Printers control panel open for the next exercise.

Exercise 9.4	Creating an Additional Logical Printer
Overview	After modifying the printer permissions and other properties in Exercise 9.3, you have found that the unauthorized use of the HPLJ5200 printer has stopped. However, you received some complaints from company executives who wanted to use the printer during a late meeting with clients and were unable to do so because it was past 5:00 PM. Some of these executives were also upset because their print jobs had to wait in the queue, just like everyone else's. As a result, you must find a way to provide selected users with unlimited, priority printer access, while still limiting the access granted to other users.
	In Exercise 9.4, you create a second printer for the same print device and use it to provide additional access to the late-working executives (whom you have added to the Administrators group on the print server computer).
Completion time	10 minutes

1. In the Devices and Printers control panel, create a new printer object for the same HP LaserJet 5200 printer connected to the computer's LPT2 port. Give the local printer the name HPLJ5200-2.

2. Share the HPLJ5200-2 printer using the share name HPLJ5200-2, configuring the Sharing tab by using the same settings you applied in Exercise 9.2.

3. Open the HPLJ5200-2 Properties sheet and click the Advanced tab.

4. Make sure the *Always available* option is selected, and change the value of the Priority spin box from 1 to 99.

Question 4	*How will modifying the Priority value help to achieve your goals?*

5.   Click Apply and then click the Security tab.

6.   In the *Group or user names* list, remove the Everyone security principal.

7.   Make sure that the Administrators group is listed as a security principal and is assigned the Print, Manage Printers, and Manage Documents permissions in the Allow column.

Question 5	How do these permission modifications help to achieve your desired goals?

8.   Close the HPLJ5200-2 Properties dialog box.

9.   Log off of the computer.

LAB CHALLENGE 9.1: CREATING A PRINTER POOL

Completion time	15 minutes

As the next phase of the printer deployment at Contoso, Ltd., the IT director has allocated five identical LaserJet 5200 printers to be used as a printer pool for the Order Entry department. Unlike the HPLJ5200 printer you installed earlier in this lab, which connected to the computer using an LPT port, these five printers all have Hewlett Packard JetDirect network interface adapters in them that have already been assigned the following IP addresses:

- 10.10.2.2
- 10.10.2.3
- 10.10.2.4
- 10.10.2.5
- 10.10.2.6

To complete this challenge, your task is to create a printer on your workstation and share it with the network using the name **HPLJ5200 OE Pool**. You must then configure the printer to function as a printer pool using the IP addresses cited earlier. Write out the procedure you used to create and configure the printer, and then take a screen shot [Alt+Prt+Scr] of the Ports tab in the HPLJ5200 OE Pool Properties sheet and paste it into your worksheet.

LAB 10
CONFIGURING
APPLICATIONS

This lab contains the following exercises and activities:

Exercise 10.1   Installing Remote Server Administration Tools

Exercise 10.2   Configuring IE8

Exercise 10.3   Using AppLocker

Lab Challenge 10.1   Suppressing Compatibility Warnings

Lab Challenge 10.2   Deploying Group Policy Objects

BEFORE YOU BEGIN

The lab environment consists of student workstations connected to a local area network, along with a server that functions as the domain controller for a domain called contoso.com. The computers required for this lab are listed in Table 10-1.

Table 10-1
Computers required for Lab 10

Computer	Operating System	Computer Name
Server	Windows Server 2008 R2	RWDC01
Workstation 1	Windows 7 Enterprise	NYC-CLa

In a classroom lab environment, there will be one classroom server and the students will have workstations named using consecutive numbers in place of the a and b variables. In a virtual lab environment, each student will have three virtual machines, named RWDC01, NYC-CL1, and NYC-CL2.

In addition to the computers, you will also require the software listed in Table 10-2 to complete Lab 10.

Table 10-2
Software required for Lab 10

Software	Location
Remote Server Administration Tools for Windows 7	\\RWDC01\dowloads\amd64fre_GRMRSATX_MSU.msu
Lab 10 student worksheet	Lab10_worksheet.rtf (provided by instructor)

This manual assumes the use of the 64-bit version of Windows 7 Enterprise. If you are working in a classroom lab that uses the 32-bit version, you must use the 32-bit version of all additional software as well.

Working with Lab Worksheets

Each lab in this manual requires that you answer questions, shoot screen shots, and perform other activities that you will document in a worksheet named for the lab, such as Lab10_worksheet.rtf. Your instructor will provide you with access to the worksheets. It is recommended that you use a USB flash drive to store your worksheets, so that you can submit them to your instructor for review. As you perform the exercises in each lab, open the appropriate worksheet file using WordPad, fill in the required information, and save the file to your flash drive.

SCENARIO

You are a Windows 7 technical specialist for Contoso, Ltd., a company with workstations in a variety of different environments. As part of your company's ongoing evaluation of Windows 7, you have been asked to explore the various methods for configuring applications in Windows 7 using Group Policy in Active Directory Domain Services (AD DS).

After completing this lab, you will be able to:

■ Install Remote Server Administration Tools

■ Configure IE8 using Group Policy

- Use AppLocker

- Configure compatibility warning policies

- Deploy a GPO

Estimated lab time: 60 minutes

Exercise 10.1	Installing Remote Server Administration Tools
Overview	Before you can configure AD DS Group Policy settings from your Windows 7 workstation, you must install and enable the Remote Server Administration Tools, which includes the Group Policy Management console.
Completion time	10 minutes

1.   Turn on the NYC-CLa workstation and log on using the **contoso\Administrator** account and the password **Pa$$w0rd**.

2.   Click Start, and in the Search programs and files box, type **\\RWDC01\dowloads\amd64fre_GRMRSATX_MSU.msu** and press Enter. A Windows Update Standalone Installer message box appears, prompting you to install an update.

3.   Click Yes. The Download and Install Updates Wizard appears, displaying the *Read these license terms* page.

4.   Click I Accept. The wizard installs the update and the *Installation complete* page appears. In addition, the Windows 7 Remote Administration Tools help file appears.

5.   Close the help file window and click Close to terminate the wizard.

6.   Click Start and then click Control Panel. The Control Panel window appears.

7.   Click Programs > Programs and Features. The Programs and Features control panel appears.

8.   Click Turn Windows features on or off. The Windows Features dialog box appears, as shown in Figure 10-1.

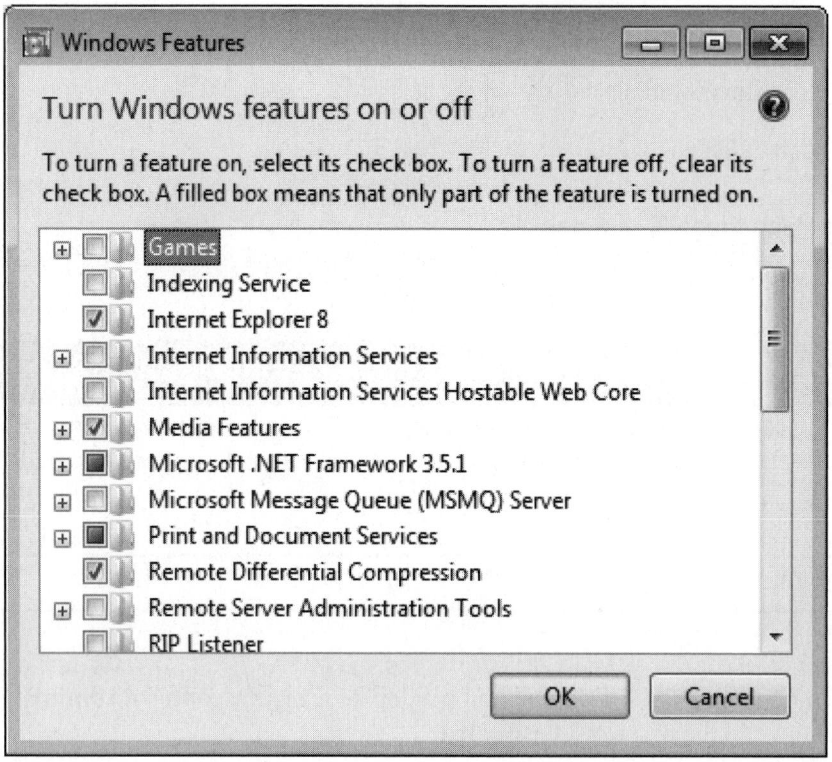

Figure 10-1
The Windows Features dialog box

9. Browse to the Remote Server Administration Tools\Feature Administration Tools container and select the Group Policy Management Tools check box. Then click OK. The system turns the selected features on.

10. Close the Programs and Features control panel.

11. Click Start. Then click Administrative Tools > Group Policy Management. The Group Policy Management console appears.

12. Browse to the Forest: contoso.com\Domains\contoso.com\Group Policy Objects container.

13. Right click the Group Policy Objects container and, from the context menu, select New. The New GPO dialog box appears.

14. In the name text box, type **NYC-CLa Policies**, where a is the number of your workstation. Then click OK. The new GPO appears in the Group Policy Objects container.

15. Take a screen shot of the Group Policy Management console, showing the GPO you created, by pressing Alt+Prt Scr, and then paste the resulting image into the Lab10_worksheet file in the page provided by pressing Ctrl+V.

Question 1	*Will the Group Policy settings you configure in your new GPO have an immediate effect on your network? Why?*

16. Leave the workstation logged on for the next exercise.

Exercise 10.2	Configuring IE8
Overview	The director of IT at Contoso, Ltd. wants to prevent the company's Windows 7 users from modifying the default Internet Explorer configuration by installing additional software, such as add-ons and accelerators. She also wants to ensure that the company intranet pages, designed several years ago for a previous IE version, display properly in IE8. Finally, the director wants to ensure that all Internet browsing activity on the network is logged for later examination. Your job is to configure the appropriate Group Policy settings to implement these requirements in your GPO.
Completion time	10 minutes

1. In the Group Policy Management console, right click the NYC-CLa Policies GPO you created in Exercise 10.1 and, from the context menu, select Edit. The Group Policy Management Editor console appears, as shown in Figure 10-2.

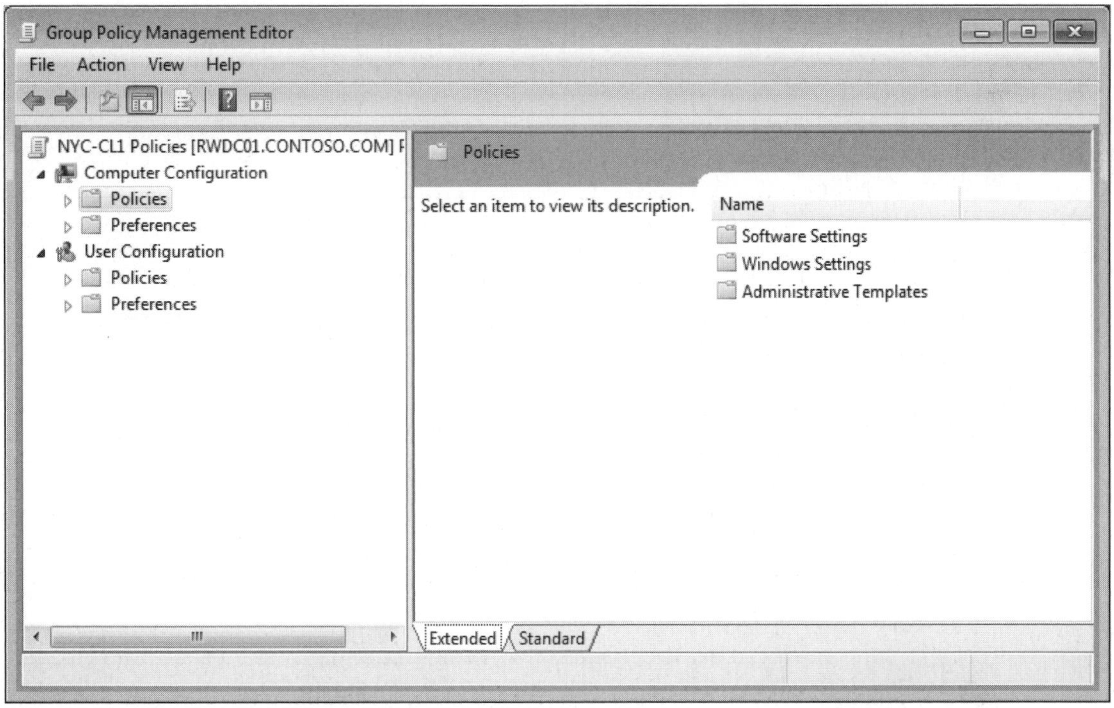

Figure 10-2
The Group Policy Management Editor console

2. Browse to the Computer Configuration\Policies\Administrative Templates\Windows Components\Internet Explorer container.

3. Double click the Do not allow users to enable or disable add-ons policy. The Do not allow users to enable or disable add-ons dialog box appears.

4. Select the *Enabled* option and click OK.

5. Select the Accelerators folder.

6. Double click the Use Policy Accelerators policy. The Use Policy Accelerators dialog box appears.

7. Select the *Enabled* option and click OK.

Question 2	*Why would you want to enable the* Use policy accelerators *policy in this case, rather than the* Turn off accelerators *policy?*

8. Select the Compatibility View container and double click the Turn on Internet Explorer Standards Mode for Local Intranet policy. The Turn on Internet Explorer Standards Mode for Local Intranet dialog box appears.

9. Select the *Disabled* option and click OK.

Question 3	*Why is it necessary to disable the Turn on Internet Explorer Standards Mode for Local Intranet policy?*

10. Select the Delete Browsing History container and double click the Prevent Deleting Web sites that the User has Visited policy. The Prevent Deleting Web sites that the User has Visited dialog box appears.

11. Select the *Enabled* option and click OK.

12. Select the InPrivate container and select the Turn off InPrivate Browsing policy. The Turn off InPrivate Browsing dialog box appears.

13. Select the *Enabled* option and click OK.

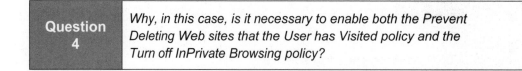

Question 4	*Why, in this case, is it necessary to enable both the Prevent Deleting Web sites that the User has Visited policy and the Turn off InPrivate Browsing policy?*

Question 5	Why isn't it necessary to enable the Turn off InPrivate Filtering as well?

14. Switch to the Group Policy Management console and expand the Group Policy Objects container.

15. Select the NYC-CLa Policies GPO and click the Settings tab. Then click Show all.

16. Take a screen shot of the Group Policy Management console displaying all of the policy settings you configured in this exercise by pressing Alt+Prt Scr, and then paste the resulting image into the Lab10_worksheet file in the page provided by pressing Ctrl+V.

17. Leave the consoles open and the computer logged on for the next exercise.

Exercise 10.3	Using AppLocker
Overview	Your IT director wants to begin using the new AppLocker feature in Windows 7 to restrict the applications that users are able to run on their workstations. She wants standard users to be able to run all of the executables included with Windows except for the Registry Editor. Members of the IT support staff, however, who are all members of the Group Policy Creator Owners group, must be able to run the Registry Editor to service other users' computers.
Completion time	10 minutes

1. In the Group Policy Management Editor console, browse to the Computer Configuration\Policies\Windows Settings\Security Settings\Application Control Policies\AppLocker container.

2. Expand the AppLocker container, as shown in Figure 10-3, and select the Executable Rules node.

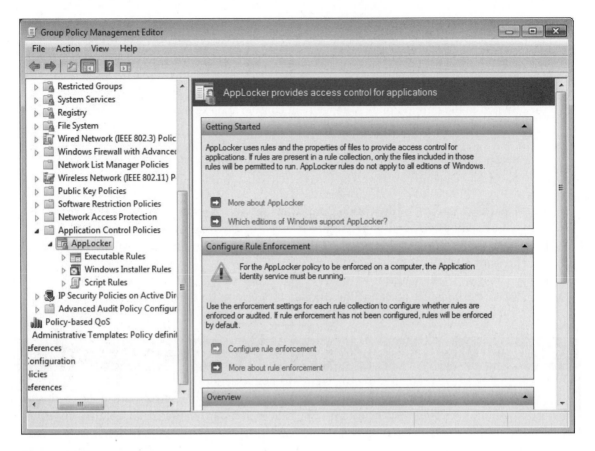

Figure 10-3
The AppLocker container in a GPO

3. Right click the Executable Rules node and, from the context menu, select Create Default Rules. Three rules appear in the Executable Rules container.

Question 6	Based on the default rules that appear in the Executable Rules folder, what programs can a typical user run on a Windows 7 workstation? What programs can members of the Administrators group run?

4. Right click the Windows Installer Rules node and, from the context menu, select Create Default Rules. Three rules appear in the Windows Installer Rules container.

Question 7	Based on the default rules that appear in the Windows Installer Rules folder, what Windows Installer files can a typical user run on a Windows 7 workstation? What Windows Installer files can members of the Administrators group run?

5. Right click the Script Rules node and, from the context menu, select Create Default Rules. Three rules appear in the Script Rules container.

6. In the Executable Rules folder, double click the All rules located in the Windows folder rule. The Allow Properties dialog box appears.

7. On the General tab, modify the Name value to **All files located in the Windows folder except Regedit**.

8. Click the Exceptions tab, and in the Add exception drop-down list, select Path.

9. Click Add. The Path Exception dialog box appears.

10. In the Path text box, type **C:\Windows\Regedit.exe** and click OK.

11. Right click the Executable Rules container and, from the context menu, select Create New Rule. The Create Executable Rules Wizard appears.

12. Click Next to bypass the *Before You Begin* page. The *Permissions* page appears.

13. Click Select. The Select User or Group dialog box appears.

14. In the Enter the object name to select box, type **Group Policy Creator Owners** and click OK. The group name appears in the User or group field on the *Permissions* page.

15. Click Next. The *Conditions* page appears.

16. Select the *Path* option and click Next. The *Path* page appears.

17. In the Path text box, type **C:\Windows\Regedit.exe** and click Create. The new rule appears in the Executable Rules container.

Question 8	Why is it necessary to create the additional rule for the Group Policy Creator Owners group?

18. Take a screen shot of the Group Policy Management Editor console displaying the contents of the Executable Rules container by pressing Alt+Prt Scr, and then paste the resulting image into the Lab10_worksheet file in the page provided by pressing Ctrl+V.

19. Leave the computer logged on for the Lab Challenge.

LAB CHALLENGE 10.1: SUPPRESSING COMPATIBILITY WARNINGS

Completion time	15 minutes

The Windows 7 users at Contoso, Ltd. are restricted to a predefined set of applications, all of which have been recently updated and carefully tested for compatibility. To prevent users from attempting to run downlevel applications, you have been instructed to disable the Windows 7 compatibility mode controls using Group Policy. To complete this challenge, you must locate and configure the appropriate Group Policy settings to accomplish these goals in the GPO you created in Exercise 10.1. Write out the procedure you used to configure the settings, and then take a screen shot of the container where the settings are located by pressing Alt+Prt Scr, and paste the resulting image into the Lab10_worksheet file in the page provided by pressing Ctrl+V.

LAB CHALLENGE 10.2: DEPLOYING GROUP POLICY OBJECTS

Completion time	15 minutes

To deploy a GPO like the one you have created in this lab, you must link it to an Active Directory Domain Services domain, site, or organizational unit object. However, for the purposes of this lab, it is necessary for the settings in your GPO to be applied to your workstation only, and not any of the other computers on the network. To complete this challenge, you must configure your GPO so that its settings apply only to the NYC-CLa computer and then link it to the contoso.com domain object in the AD DS tree. Write out the procedure you used to complete the challenge, and then take a screen shot showing the configuration that limits the scope of the GPO by pressing Alt+Prt Scr, and paste the resulting image into the Lab10_worksheet file in the page provided by pressing Ctrl+V

LAB 11
MANAGING AND MONITORING PERFORMANCE

This lab contains the following exercises and activities:

Exercise 11.1   Using Event Viewer

Exercise 11.2   Creating Event Subscriptions

Exercise 11.3   Using Performance Monitor

Exercise 11.4   Logging Performance Data

Lab Challenge 11.1   Viewing a Performance Counter Log

BEFORE YOU BEGIN

The lab environment consists of student workstations connected to a local area network, along with a server that functions as the domain controller for a domain called contoso.com. The computers required for this lab are listed in Table 11-1.

Table 11-1
Computers required for Lab 11

Computer	Operating System	Computer Name
Server	Windows Server 2008 R2	RWDC01
Workstation 1	Windows 7 Enterprise	NYC-CLa
Workstation 2	Windows 7 Enterprise	NYC-CLb

>
> **NOTE**
> *In a classroom lab environment, there will be one classroom server and the students will have workstations named using consecutive numbers in place of the a and b variables. In a virtual lab environment, each student will have three virtual machines, named RWDC01, NYC-CL1, and NYC-CL2.*

In addition to the computers, you will also require the software listed in Table 11-2 to complete Lab 11.

Table 11-2
Software required for Lab 11

Software	Location
Lab 11 student worksheet	Lab11_worksheet.rtf (provided by instructor)

Working with Lab Worksheets

Each lab in this manual requires that you answer questions, shoot screen shots, and perform other activities that you will document in a worksheet named for the lab, such as Lab11_worksheet.rtf. Your instructor will provide you with access to the worksheets. It is recommended that you use a USB flash drive to store your worksheets, so that you can submit them to your instructor for review. As you perform the exercises in each lab, open the appropriate worksheet file using WordPad, fill in the required information, and save the file to your flash drive.

SCENARIO

You are a newly hired desktop technician for Contoso, Ltd. and have been assigned to work on a long-term test deployment of some new Windows 7 workstations. Your job is to track the computers' performance levels over the course of a week and determine which components, if any, are negatively affecting system performance.

After completing this lab, you will be able to:

- Create filters, custom views, and subscriptions in the Event Viewer console

- Monitor system performance using the Performance Monitor console

Estimated lab time: 70 minutes

Exercise 11.1	Using Event Viewer
Overview	In Exercise 11.1, you demonstrate some methods for isolating the most important events in the Windows 7 logs.
Completion time	10 minutes

1. Turn on the NYC-CLa workstation and log on using the **contoso\Administrator** account and the password **Pa$$w0rd**.

2. Click Start. Then click Administrative Tools > Event Viewer. The Event Viewer console appears, as shown in Figure 11-1.

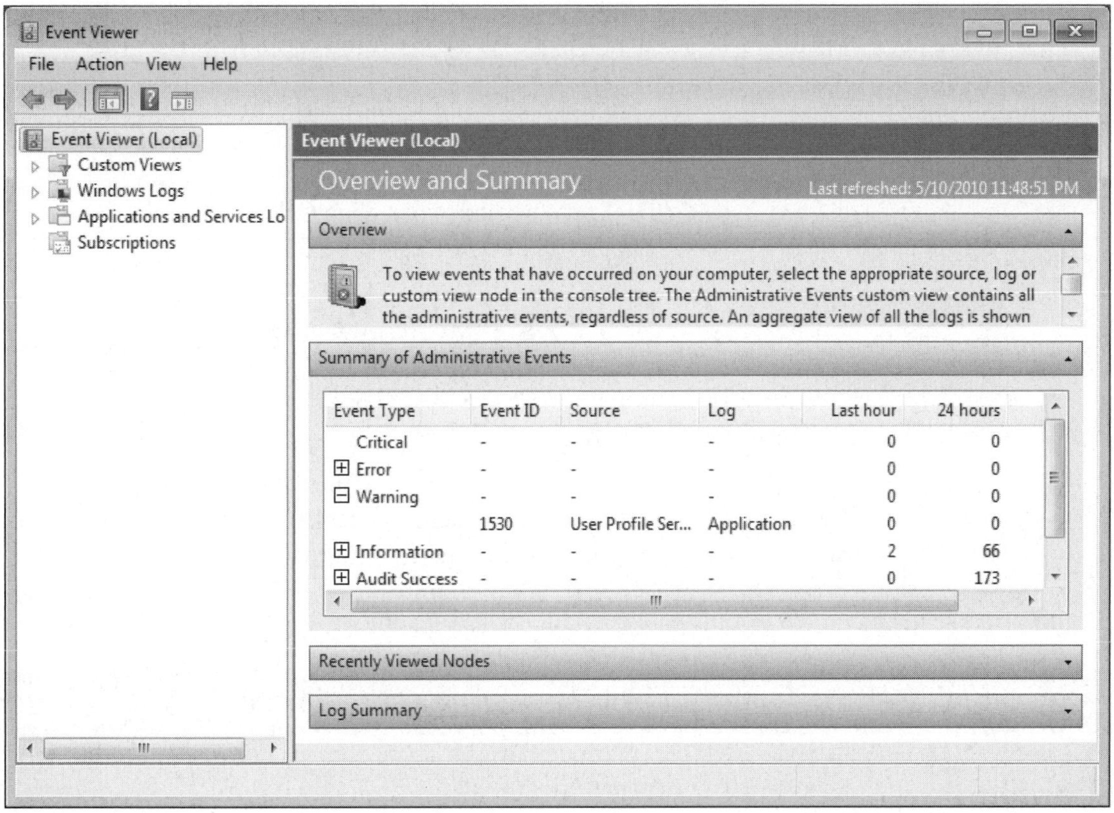

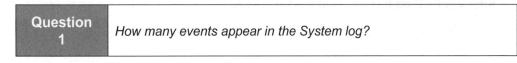

Figure 11-1
The Event Viewer console

3. Expand the Windows Logs folder and select the System log. The contents of the log appear in the detail pane.

> | **Question 1** | *How many events appear in the System log?* |

4. From the Action menu, select Filter Current Log. The Filter Current Log dialog box appears.

5. In the Event level area, select the Critical and Warning check boxes. Then click OK.

> | **Question 2** | *How many events appear in the System log now?* |

6.   From the Action menu, select Create Custom View. The Create Custom View dialog box appears.

7.   In the Logged drop-down list, select *Last 7 days*.

8.   In the Event level area, select the Critical and Warning check boxes.

9.   Leave the *By log* option selected and, in the *Event logs* drop-down list, select the Application, Security, and System check boxes.

10.   Click OK. The Save Filter to Custom View dialog box appears.

11.   In the Name text box, type **Critical & Warning**. Then click OK. The Critical & Warning view you just created appears in the Custom Views folder.

Question 3	How many events appear in the Critical & Warning custom view?

12.   Take a screen shot of the Event Viewer console, showing the Critical & Warning custom view, by pressing Ctrl+Prt Scr and then paste the resulting image into the Lab11_worksheet file in the page provided by pressing Ctrl+V.

13.   Leave the Event Viewer console open for the next exercise.

Exercise 11.2	Creating Event Subscriptions
Overview	In Exercise 11.2, you demonstrate some methods for isolating the most important events in the Windows 7 logs.
Completion time	20 minutes

NOTE	In a classroom lab environment, students should work with a partner so that they have one workstation functioning as the event collector and one workstation functioning as the event source.

1.   Turn on the NYC-CLb workstation and log on using the **contoso\Administrator** account and the password **Pa$$w0rd**.

2.   Click Start, then click All Programs > Accessories. Right click Command Prompt and, from the context menu, select *Run as administrator*. An Administrator: Command Prompt window appears.

3.   In the Command Prompt window, type **winrm quickconfig** and press Enter.

4.   Press **y** at each of the prompts until the command completes.

5.   On the NYC-CLa workstation, click Start, then click All Programs >
     Accessories. Right click Command Prompt and, from the context menu, select
     Run as administrator. An Administrator: Command Prompt window appears.

6.   In the Command Prompt window, type **wecutil qc** and press Enter.

7.   Press **y** at the prompt to complete the command.

8.   In the Event Viewer console, select the Subscriptions node.

9.   Right click Subscriptions and, from the context menu, select Create Subscription.
     The Subscription Properties dialog box appears, as shown in Figure 11-2.

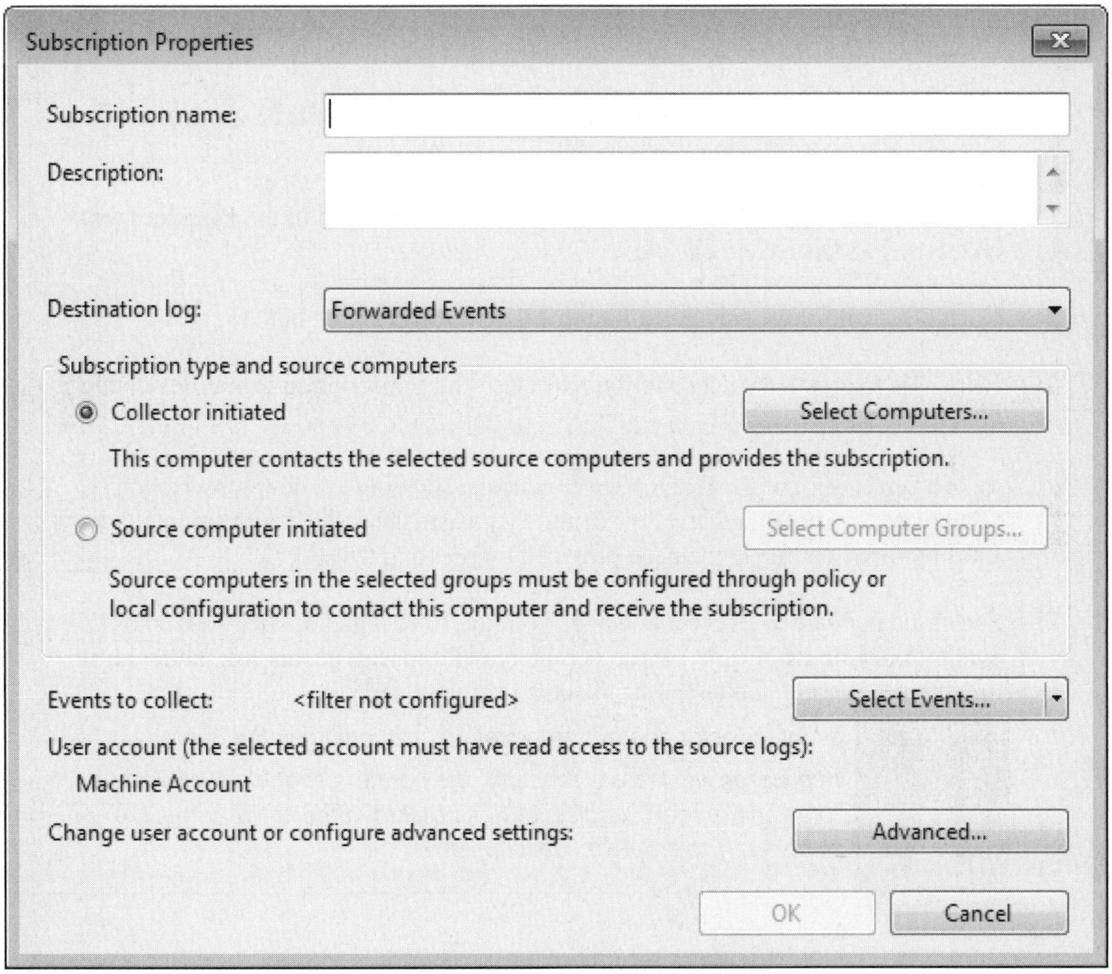

Figure 11-2
The Subscription Properties dialog box

10.   In the Subscription name text box, type **NYC-CLb**, where b is the number of the
      other workstation.

11. Select the *Collector initiated* option and click Select Computers. The Computers dialog box appears.

12. Click Add Domain Computers. The Select Computers dialog box appears.

13. In the *Enter the object name to select* box, type **NYC-CLb** and click OK. The computer appears in the Computers dialog box.

14. Click OK.

15. In the Subscription Properties dialog box, click Select Events. The Query Filter dialog box appears.

16. Select all five of the *Event level* check boxes and, in the *Event logs* drop-down list, select the System check box. Then, click OK.

17. Click Advanced. The Advanced Subscription Settings dialog box appears.

18. Select the Specific User option and click *User and Password*. The Credentials for Subscription Source dialog box appears.

19. In the *User name* text box, type **contoso\Administrator** and in the Password text box, type **Pa$$w0rd** and click OK.

20. Click OK to close the Advanced Subscription Settings dialog box.

21. Click OK to create the subscription and close the Subscription Properties dialog box.

22. Take a screen shot of the Event Viewer console, showing the new subscription you created, by pressing Ctrl+Prt Scr and then paste the resulting image into the Lab11_worksheet file in the page provided by pressing Ctrl+V.

23. Select the Forwarded Events node and, from the Action menu, click Refresh. The events forwarded from the source computer will appear in this log, although it might take several minutes for the events to begin to appear.

In a classroom lab environment, the partners should now switch roles and repeat Exercise 11.2, so that the other partner has the opportunity to create a subscription.

24. Leave the computer logged on for the next exercise.

Exercise 11.3   Using Performance Monitor

Overview	The technical specialists at Contoso, Ltd. routinely use the Performance Monitor tool to examine the performance levels of Windows 7 workstations. However, each technician uses Performance Monitor in a different way. The IT director wants to create a standard set of performance counters that are easily visible in a single Performance Monitor line graph, which would enable the support staff to compare the performance levels of different computer models. You have been given the task of selecting the performance counters for this standard Performance Monitor configuration and testing their visibility on the graph.
Completion time	15 minutes

1. On the NYC-CLa workstation, click Start, and then click Control Panel. The Control Panel window appears.

2. Click System and Security > Administrative Tools. Then click Performance Monitor. The Performance Monitor console appears.

3. Browse to Monitoring Tools\Performance Monitor. The default Performance Monitor window appears, as shown in Figure 11-3.

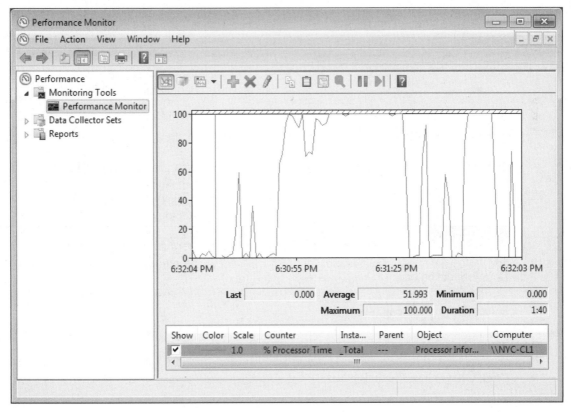

Figure 11-3
The Performance Monitor console

Question 4	What counter appears in the Performance Monitor display by default?

4. Remove the default counter from the Performance Monitor graph by selecting it in the legend (below the line graph) and clicking the Delete button in the toolbar.

5. Click the Add button in the toolbar. The Add Counters dialog box appears.

6. In the Available Counters list, expand the Server Work Queues entry, as shown in Figure 11-4.

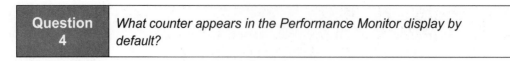

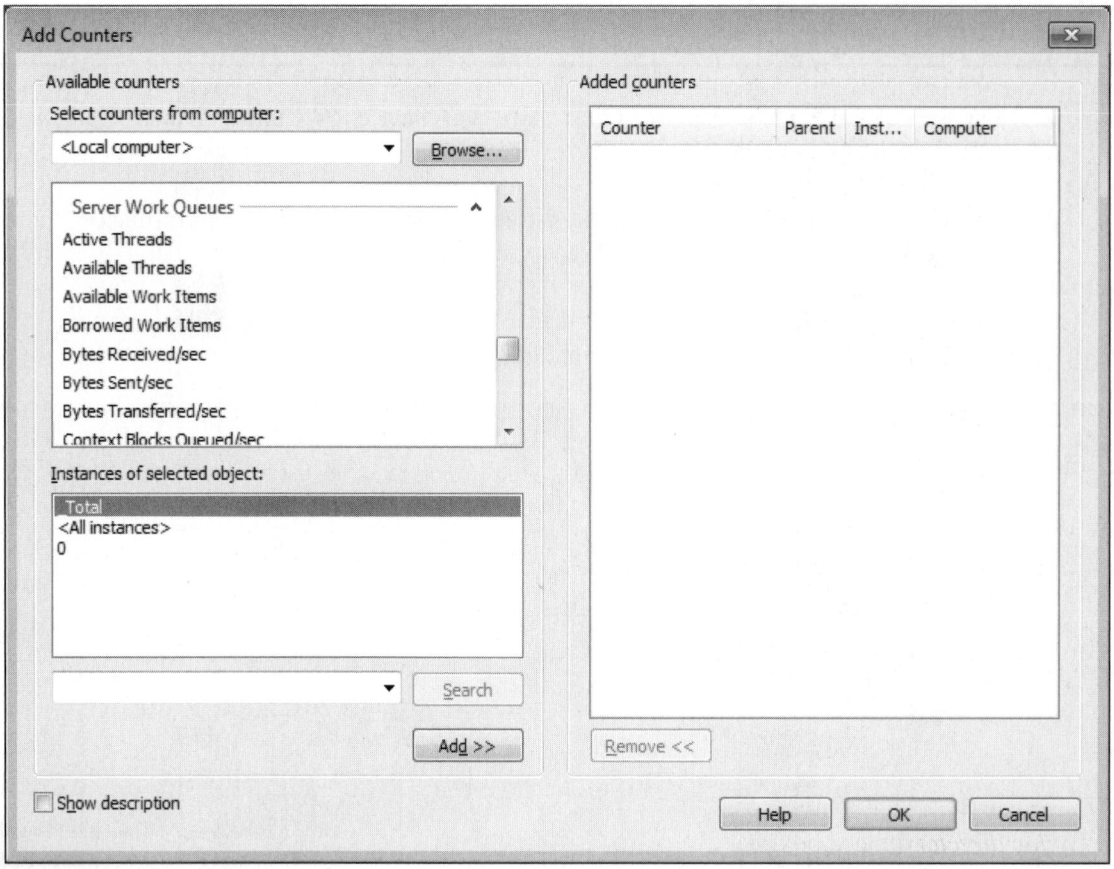

Figure 11-4
The Add Counters dialog box

7. Select the Queue Length counter.

8. In the *Instances of selected object* list, select 0, and then click Add.

9. Click OK to close the dialog box.

Question 5	What happens?

10. Using the same process, add the following additional counters to the graph:

- System: Processor Queue Length
- Memory: Page Faults/Sec
- Memory: Pages/Sec
- PhysicalDisk (_Total): Current Disk Queue Length

NOTE	*For each of the performance counters listed, the first term (before the colon) is the name of the performance object in which the counter is located. The second term (after the colon) is the name of the counter itself. A value in parentheses appearing after the performance object name (immediately before the colon) is the instance of the counter.*

11. Click OK to close the Add Counters dialog box.

Question 6	*Does this selection of counters make for an effective graph? Why or why not?*

Question 7	*How would using the report view instead of the line graph view affect the compatibility of the performance counters you select?*

12. Minimize the Performance Monitor console and launch any three new programs from the Start menu.

13. Maximize the Performance Monitor console.

Question 8	*What effect does launching the programs have on the Performance Monitor graph?*

14. Take a screen shot of the Performance Monitor console showing the line graph by pressing Alt+Prt Scr, and then paste the resulting image into the Lab11_worksheet file in the page provided by pressing Ctrl+V.

15. Click the Properties button on the toolbar. The Performance Monitor Properties sheet appears.

16. Click the Graph tab, as shown in Figure 11-5.

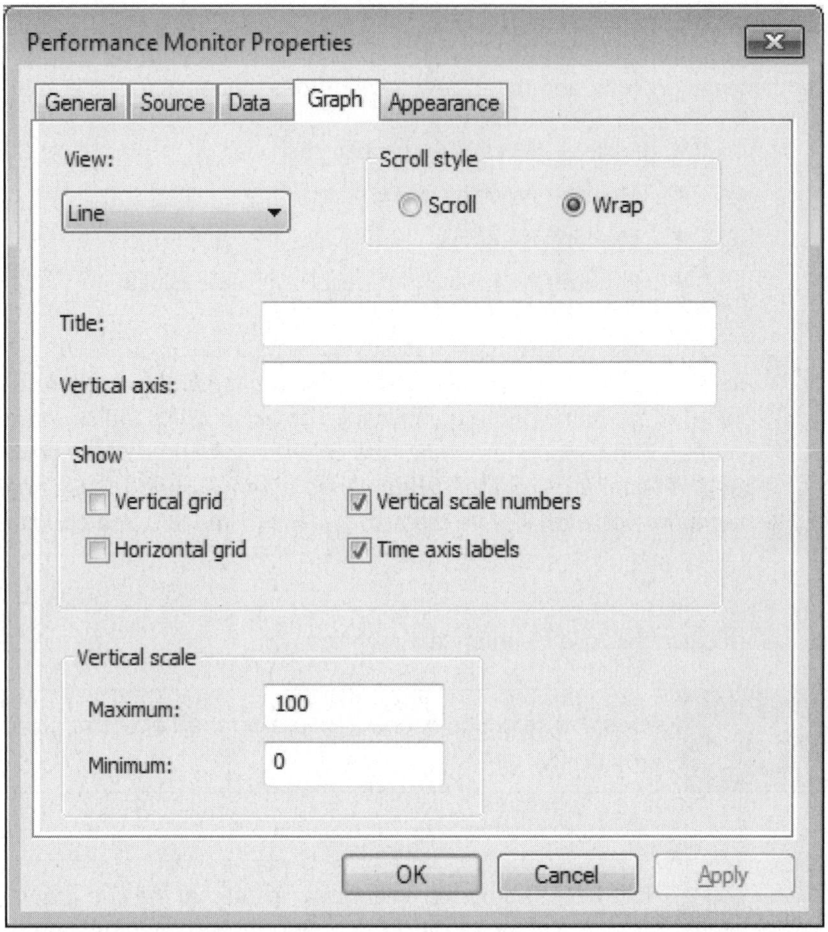

Figure 11-5
The Graph tab of the Performance Monitor Properties sheet

17. In the Vertical scale box, change the value of the Maximum field to 200 and click OK.

Question 9	Does this modification make the graph easier or more difficult to read? Why or why not?

18. From the console's Window menu, select New Window. A new Console Root window appears.

19. Display the Performance Monitor graph in the new window.

20. Click the Add button, and add the following counters to the Performance Monitor graph:

   - Network Interface (All Instances): Packets/Sec
   - Network Interface (All Instances): Output Queue Length
   - Server: Bytes Total/Sec

21. Click OK to close the Add Counters dialog box.

Question 10	*Does this selection of counters make for an effective graph? Why or why not?*

22. Leave the Performance Monitor console open for the next exercise.

Exercise 11.4	Logging Performance Data
Overview	To properly gauge the performance level of a computer, it is helpful to have a baseline reading that you've taken under normal operating conditions that you can use to compare with the levels when the computer is under the stress of a workload. You have been given the task of taking baseline performance level readings on a new computer using the Performance Monitor console. In Exercise 11.4, you use the Data Collector Sets tool to create a counter log for the computer, saving the baseline levels to a file for later examination.
Completion time	15 minutes

1. In the Performance Monitor console, expand the Data Collector Sets node and select the User Defined container.

2. Right click the User Defined container, point to New, and select Data Collector Set. The Create New Data Collector Set Wizard appears, as shown in Figure 11-6.

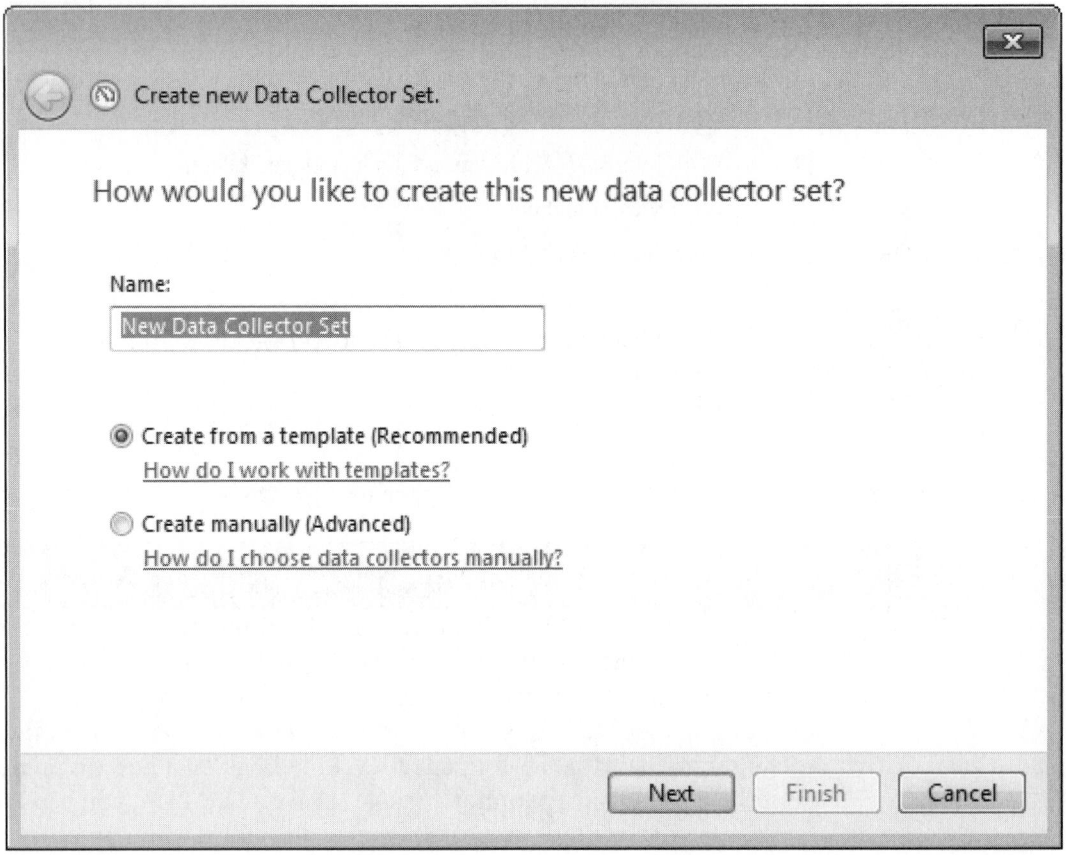

Figure 11-6
The Create New Data Collector Set Wizard

3.   In the Name text box, type **NYC-CLa Baseline**, where a is the number assigned to your workstation.

4.   Select the Create manually (Advanced) option and click Next. The *What type of data do you want to include?* page appears.

5.   With the Create Data Logs option selected, select the Performance counter check box and click Next. The *Which performance counters would you like to log?* page appears.

6.   Click the Add button. The Available Counters dialog box appears.

7.   Using the same procedure as in Exercise 11-3, add the following counters:

- Processor (_Total): % Processor time
- Processor (_Total): Interrupts/Sec
- System: Processor Queue Length
- Server Work Queues (0): Queue Length
- Memory: Page Faults/Sec
- Memory: Pages/Sec

- Memory: Available Bytes
- Memory: Committed Bytes
- Memory: Pool Nonpaged Bytes
- PhysicalDisk (_Total): Disk Bytes/Sec
- PhysicalDisk (_Total): Avg. Disk Bytes/Transfer
- PhysicalDisk (_Total): Current Disk Queue Length
- PhysicalDisk (_Total): % Disk Time
- LogicalDisk (_Total): % Free Space
- Network Interface (All Instances): Bytes Total/Sec
- Network Interface (All Instances): Output Queue Length
- Server: Bytes Total/Sec

8. Click OK to close the Add Counters dialog box.

9. Take a screen shot of the *Which performance counters would you like to log?* page by pressing Alt+Prt Scr, and then paste the resulting image into the Lab11_worksheet file in the page provided by pressing Ctrl+V.

10. Set the Sample Interval value to 10 and the units value to Seconds, and then click Next. The *Where would you like the data to be saved?* page appears.

11. Click Next to accept the default location. The *Create the data collector set?* page appears.

12. Select the Open properties for this data collector set option and click Finish. The NYC-CLa Baseline Properties sheet appears, as shown in Figure 11-7.

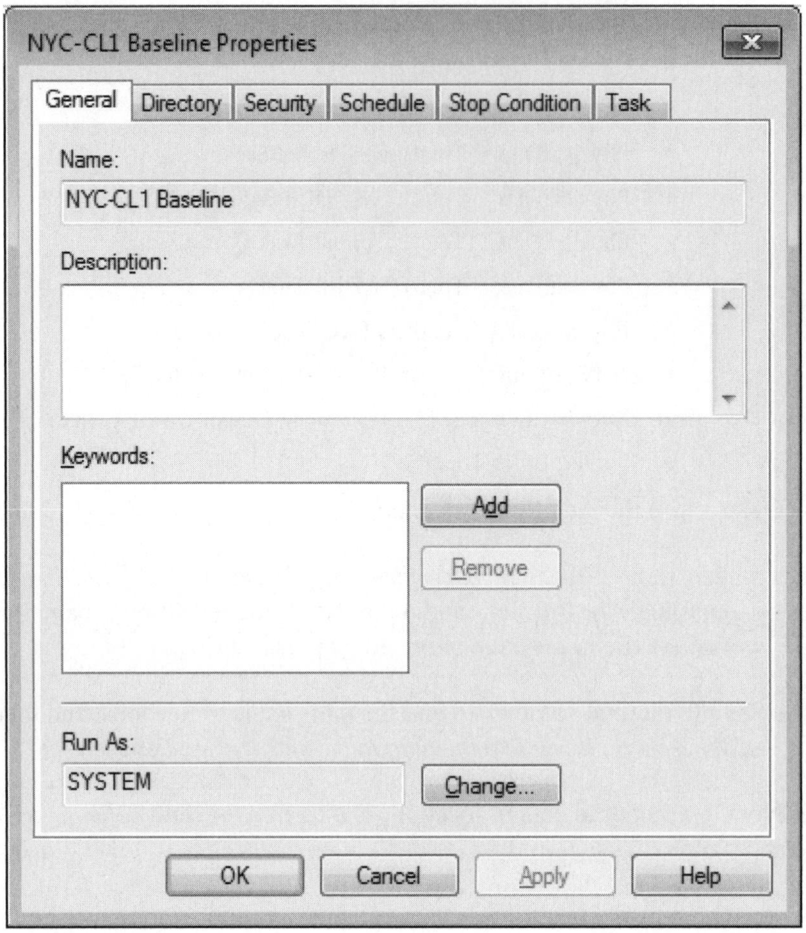

Figure 11-7
The NYC-CLa Baseline Properties sheet

Question 11	*When creating a performance counter data collector set, under what circumstances would it be necessary to specify a username and password in the Run As section of the collector set's Properties sheet?*

13. Click the Schedule tab, and then click Add. The Folder Action dialog box appears.

14. Make sure that today's date appears in the Beginning date drop-down list.

15. Select the Expiration date check box, and make sure that today's date appears in the drop-down list.

16. In the Launch box, set the Start time value for five minutes from now. Clear all of the check boxes except the one for the current day of the week, and then click OK.

17. Click the Stop Condition tab.

18. Select the Overall Duration check box, set the value for **10 minutes**, and then click OK.

19. The NYC-CLa Baseline data collector set appears in the console.

Question 12	*What happens when the Start Time you configured arrives?*

20. Wait 10 minutes for the logging process to complete.

21. Leave the Performance Monitor console open.

LAB CHALLENGE 11.1: VIEWING A PERFORMANCE COUNTER LOG

Completion time	10 minutes

In Exercise 11.4, you created a performance counter data collector set for the purpose of gathering baseline performance data for your Windows 7 workstation. To complete this challenge, you must use the Performance Monitor console to display the data you gathered for the counters in the Memory performance object that you collected. Write out the procedure you used to display the data and take a screen shot of the console showing the collector set data by pressing Alt+Prt Scr, and then paste the resulting image into the Lab11_worksheet file in the page provided by pressing Ctrl+V.

LAB 12
WORKING WITH WORKGROUPS AND DOMAINS

This lab contains the following exercises and activities:

BEFORE YOU BEGIN

The lab environment consists of student workstations connected to a local area network, along with a server that functions as the domain controller for a domain called contoso.com. The computers required for this lab are listed in Table 12-1.

Table 12-1
Computers required for Lab 12

Computer	Operating System	Computer Name
Server	Windows Server 2008 R2	RWDC01
Workstation 1	Windows 7 Enterprise	NYC-CLa

NOTE	In a classroom lab environment, there will be one classroom server and the students will have workstations named using consecutive numbers in place of the a and b variables. In a virtual lab environment, each student will have three virtual machines, named RWDC01, NYC-CL1, and NYC-CL2.

In addition to the computers, you will also require the software listed in Table 12-2 to complete Lab 12.

Table 12-2
Software required for Lab 12

Software	Location
Remote Server Administration Tools for Windows 7	Already installed in Exercise 10.1
Lab 12 student worksheet	Lab12_worksheet.rtf (provided by instructor)

Working with Lab Worksheets

Each lab in this manual requires that you answer questions, shoot screen shots, and perform other activities that you will document in a worksheet named for the lab, such as Lab12_worksheet.rtf. Your instructor will provide you with access to the worksheets. It is recommended that you use a USB flash drive to store your worksheets, so that you can submit them to your instructor for review. As you perform the exercises in each lab, open the appropriate worksheet file using WordPad, fill in the required information, and save the file to your flash drive.

SCENARIO

You are a Windows 7 technical specialist for Contoso, Ltd., a company with workstations in a variety of different environments. Some of the Windows 7 computers are members of a workgroup, while others are members of an Active Directory domain. You have been assigned the task of creating user and group accounts for new employees that the company has recently hired and assigning them the privileges they need to access various company resources. Because of the differing system configurations, the procedures for creating the users and groups vary.

After completing this lab, you will be able to:

- Join workstations to workgroups and domains

- Create local users and groups

- Create domain users and groups using Net.exe

Estimated lab time: 75 minutes

Exercise 12.1 Joining a Workgroup

Overview	In Exercise 12.1, you configure your workstation as a member of a workgroup, so that you can use all of the Windows 7 tools for creating local users and groups.
Completion time	10 minutes

> **NOTE**
>
> *In the default lab environment, all workstations are joined to an Active Directory Domain Services domain. It is therefore necessary to remove the workstation from the domain and join it to a workgroup before you can complete the upcoming exercises.*

1. Turn on the NYC-CLa workstation and log on using the **contoso\Administrator** account and the password **Pa$$w0rd**.

2. Click Start. Then click Control Panel. The Control Panel window appears.

3. Click System and Security > System. The System control panel appears, as shown in Figure 12-1.

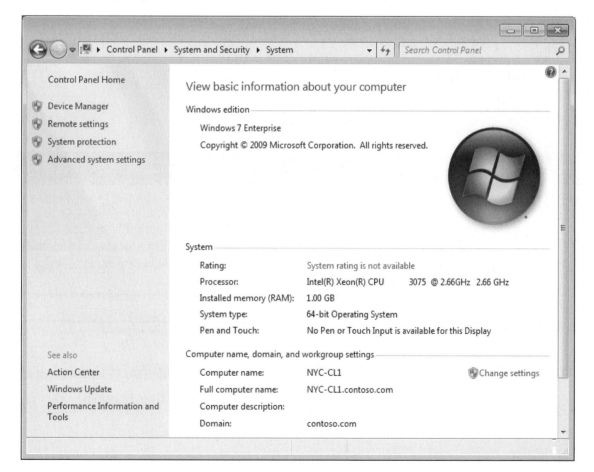

Figure 12-1
The System control panel

4.   Click Change settings. The System Properties sheet appears.

5.   On the Computer Name tab, click Change. The Computer Name/Domain Changes dialog box appears.

6.   Select the Workgroup option and in the text box, type **Workgroup** and click OK. A Computer Name/Domain Changes message box appears, reminding you that you will need the local administrator password to log on.

7.   Click OK. A Computer Name/Domain Changes message box appears, welcoming you to the workgroup.

8.   Take a screen shot showing the Welcome message by pressing Ctrl+Prt Scr and then paste the resulting image into the Lab12_worksheet file in the page provided by pressing Ctrl+V.

9.   Click OK. A Computer Name/Domain Changes message box appears, reminding you to restart the computer.

10.   Click OK. Then click Close to close the System Properties sheet. A Microsoft Windows message box appears, reminding you again to restart the computer.

11.   Click Restart Now. The computer restarts.

12.   Log on to the workstation using the **NYC-CLa\Administrator** account and the password **Pa$$w0rd**.

13.   Leave the computer logged on for the next exercise.

Exercise 12.2	Creating Local Users and Groups
Overview	The new hires in the Accounting department at Contoso, Ltd. need local user accounts for their workgroup computers—not only for themselves, but also for other department workers who need access to their data. In Exercise 12.2, you create a new local user account for the director of the accounting department, Jay Adams, using the Windows 7 User Accounts control panel.
Completion time	15 minutes

1.   Click Start. Then click Control Panel. The Control Panel window appears.

2.   Click User Accounts and Family Safety > User Accounts. The User Accounts control panel appears, as shown in Figure 12-2.

Figure 12-2
The User Accounts control panel

3.   Click Manage another account. The *Choose the account you would like to change* page appears.

4.   Click Create a new account. The *Name the account and choose an account type* page appears.

5.   In the *New account name* text box, type **JAdams**. Leave the Standard User option selected and click Create Account. The JAdams account is added to the *Choose the account you would like to change* page.

6.   Click the JAdams account you just created. The *Make changes to JAdams's account* page appears.

7.   Click Change the password. The *Change JAdams's password* page appears.

8.   In the *New password* and *Confirm new password* text boxes, type **pass** and click Change password.

9.   A User Account Control Panel message box appears, informing you that the password you typed does not meet password policy requirements.

10.   Click OK to continue.

Question 1	In what way(s) did the password you tried to use not meet the password policy requirements?

11. Try to set the password for the JAdams account using the passwords in Table 12-3. For each password that fails, explain why it failed in the space provided in your worksheet. Once you successfully set the password, the *Make changes to JAdams's account* page re-appears.

Table 12-3
Proposed passwords

Password	Reason for Failure
Smadaj	
jadams000	
Jadams1!	
Password	
Pa$$w0rd	

12. Click Manage another account. The *Choose the user account you would like to change* page appears.

13. Take a screen shot of the *Choose the user account you would like to change* page with the new account you created by pressing Ctrl+Prt Scr, and then paste the resulting image into the Lab12_worksheet file in the page provided by pressing Ctrl+V.

14. Close the User Accounts Control Panel.

15. Leave the computer logged on for the next exercise.

Exercise 12.3	Using the Local Users and Groups Snap-In
Overview	You have discovered that while the User Accounts screen makes it easy to create accounts for local users, it does not provide access to all of the user account properties you need to secure the computer. Therefore, you decide to create the rest of the local accounts for the computer using the Local Users and Groups snap-in for Microsoft Management Console (MMC) instead.
Completion time	15 minutes

1. Click Start. Then click Control Panel. The Control Panel window appears.

2. Click System And Security > Administrative Tools. The Administrative Tools window appears.

3. Double click Computer Management. The Computer Management console appears.

4. Expand the Local Users and Groups folder and select the Users subfolder. A list of user accounts on the computer appears, as shown in Figure 12-3.

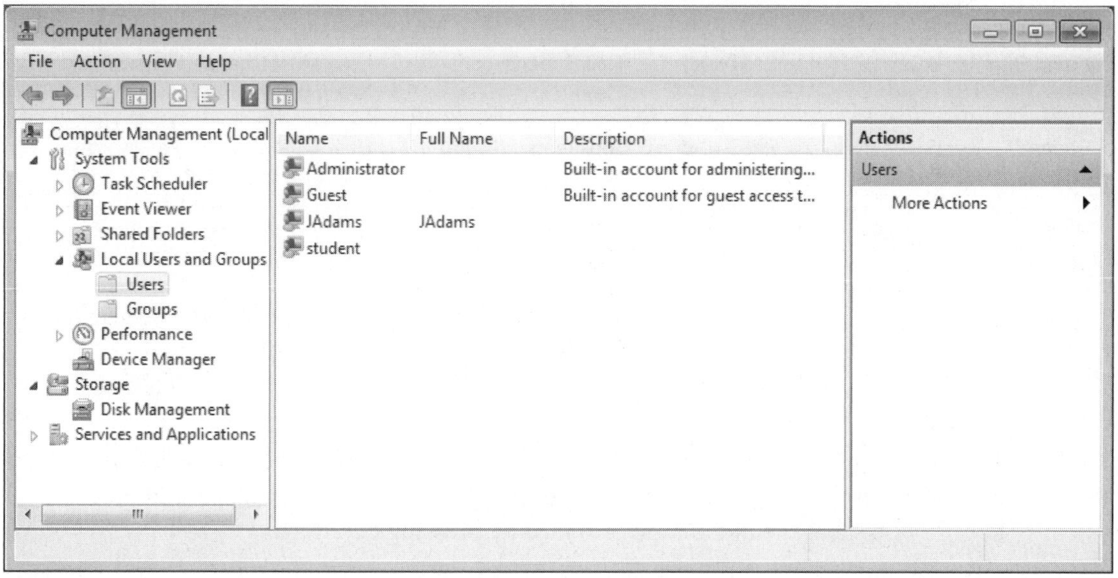

Figure 12-3
The Local Users and Groups snap-in

5. Double click the JAdams user account. The JAdams Properties dialog box appears.

Question 2	*What tasks can you perform in the JAdams Properties dialog box that you could not perform in the User Accounts control panel?*

6. In the Full Name text box, type **Jay Adams**. Make sure the *Password never expires* check box is clear. Select the *User must change password at next logon* check box and then click OK.

7. Right click the Users folder and, from the context menu, select New User. The New User dialog box appears.

8. Create the user accounts listed in Table 12-4 and include the specified properties.

Table 12-4
New local user information

Full Name	Account Name	Password	Position	Selected Check Boxes
Pilar Ackerman	PAckerman	Pa$$w0rd	Bookkeeper (Day)	User Must Change Password At Next Logon
Adam Barr	ABarr	Pa$$w0rd	Shift Supervisor (Day)	User Must Change Password At Next Logon
Susan Metters	SMetters	Pa$$w0rd	Bookkeeper (Night)	User Must Change Password At Next Logon
Heidi Steen	HSteen	Pa$$w0rd	Shift Supervisor (Night)	User Must Change Password At Next Logon
Tai Yee	TYee	Pa$$w0rd	Administrative Assistant	User Must Change Password At Next Logon

9. Take a screen shot of the Computer Management console with the new accounts you created by pressing Ctrl+Prt Scr, and then paste the resulting image into the Lab12_worksheet file in the page provided by pressing Ctrl+V.

10. Leave the Computer Management console open for the next exercise.

Exercise 12.4	Managing Group Memberships
Overview	When you create local user accounts with the User Accounts control panel, you have two account type options (Standard User and Administrator) to choose from that are actually a means of creating memberships in the Users and Administrators groups, respectively. In the Local Users and Groups snap-in, you must manually configure the group memberships for the new users.
	The IT director of Contoso, Ltd. has ordered that every workgroup computer have two additional local groups created on it, called Accounting and Bookkeeping. She has also provided you with the following group membership assignments that must be implemented on every workgroup computer.
	<ul><li>Accounting—Director, shift supervisors, administrative assistants</li><li>Bookkeeping—Director, bookkeepers, administrative assistants</li><li>Administrators—Director, shift supervisors</li><li>Power Users—Director, bookkeepers</li><li>Users—Director, shift supervisors, bookkeepers, administrative assistants</li></ul>
Completion time	10 minutes

1. In the Computer Management console, click the Groups folder.

Question 3	How many built-in local groups are there on the computer?

2. Right click the Groups folder and, from the context menu, select New Group. The New Group dialog box appears.

3. In the *Group name* text box, type **Accounting** and click Create. After creating the group, the dialog box resets itself.

4. In the *Group name* text box, type **Bookkeeping**. Click Create, and then click Close.

5. Take a screen shot of the Computer Management console showing the contents of the Groups folder by pressing Ctrl+Prt Scr, and then paste the resulting image into the Lab12_worksheet file in the page provided by pressing Ctrl+V.

6. In the Users folder, open the Properties dialog box for the JAdams account you created in Exercise 12.2 and click the Member of tab.

Question 4	Of which group(s) is Jay Adams currently a member?

7. Click Add. The Select Groups dialog box appears.

8. In the *Enter the object names to select* text box, type **Accounting; Bookkeeping; Administrators; Power Users**. Click Check Names, and then click OK. The groups appear in the Member of list.

9. Click OK to close the JAdams Properties dialog box.

10. Using the account information in Table 12-4 and the membership assignments at the beginning of this exercise, create the appropriate group memberships for all of the users you created in Exercise 12.3.

11. Close the Computer Management console.

Exercise 12.5	Joining a Domain
Overview	Now that you have created the new local user accounts and group memberships on the workstation, you will rejoin the computer to the contoso.com domain, so that you can work with domain users and groups. You must also enable the Active Directory Users and Computers console, provided with the Remote Server Administration Tools package installed earlier.
Completion time	10 minutes

> **NOTE** *In a classroom lab environment, this exercise assumes that you have already completed Exercise 10.1, in which you installed the Remote Server Administration Tools for Windows 7 package. If you have not completed Exercise 10.1, you must do so before you can complete this exercise.*

1. Click Start. Then click Control Panel. The Control Panel window appears.

2. Click System and Security > System. The System control panel appears.

3. Click Change Settings. The System Properties sheet appears.

4. On the Computer Name tab, click Change. The Computer Name/Domain Changes dialog box appears.

5. Select the Domain option and in the text box, type **contoso.com** and click OK. A Windows Security dialog box appears.

6. In the User name text box, type **Administrator** and in the Password text box, type **Pa$$w0rd**. Then click OK. A Computer Name/Domain Changes message box appears, welcoming you to the domain.

7. Take a screen shot showing the Welcome message by pressing Ctrl+Prt Scr and then paste the resulting image into the Lab12_worksheet file in the page provided by pressing Ctrl+V.

8. Click OK. A Computer Name/Domain Changes message box appears, reminding you to restart the computer.

9. Click OK. Then click Close to close the System Properties sheet. A Microsoft Windows message box appears, reminding you again to restart the computer.

10. Click Restart Now. The computer restarts.

11. Log on to the workstation using the **contoso\Administrator** account and the password **Pa$$w0rd.**

12. Click Start. Then click Control Panel. The Control Panel window appears.

13. Click Programs > Programs and Features. Then click Turn Windows features on or off. The Windows Features dialog box appears.

14. Browse to the Remote Server Administration Tools\Role Administration Tools\AD DS and AD LDS Tools\AD DS Tools container and select the AD DS Snap-ins and Command-Line Tools check box. Then click OK.

15. Leave the computer logged on.

LAB CHALLENGE 12.1: CREATING DOMAIN USERS AND GROUPS

Completion time	15 minutes

In Exercises 12.2, 12.3, and 12.4, you created several local user accounts and two local groups, and then added the users as members of the appropriate groups. To complete this challenge, you must complete the same tasks by creating domain users and groups using the Net.exe command line utility. Write a list of Net.exe commands that will create a user account for the Director Jay Adams (JAdams), the users from Table 12-4, and the groups from Exercise 12.4, and then add the users to the correct groups, according to the following assignments:

- Accounting—Director, shift supervisors, administrative assistants
- Bookkeeping—Director, bookkeepers, administrative assistants
- Domain Admins—Director, shift supervisors
- Enterprise Admins—Director
- Domain Users—Director, shift supervisors, bookkeepers, administrative assistants

When you are finished, open an elevated command prompt on your workstation and execute the commands. Then open the Active Directory Users and Computer console and take a screen shot of the console, showing the users and groups you created.

LAB 13
CONFIGURING
SECURITY SETTINGS

This lab contains the following exercises and activities:

Exercise 13.1   Installing Internet Information Server

Exercise 13.2   Testing IIS Connectivity

Exercise 13.3   Allowing a Program through the Firewall

Exercise 13.4   Creating Windows Firewall Rules

BEFORE YOU BEGIN

The lab environment consists of student workstations connected to a local area network, along with a server that functions as the domain controller for a domain called contoso.com. The computers required for this lab are listed in Table 13-1.

Table 13-1
Computers required for Lab 13

Computer	Operating System	Computer Name
Server	Windows Server 2008 R2	RWDC01
Workstation 1	Windows 7 Enterprise	NYC-CLa
Workstation 2	Windows 7 Enterprise	NYC-CLb

NOTE

In a classroom lab environment, there will be one classroom server and the students will have workstations named using consecutive numbers in place of the a and b variables. In a virtual lab environment, each student will have three virtual machines, named RWDC01, NYC-CL1, and NYC-CL2.

In addition to the computers, you will also require the software listed in Table 13-2 to complete Lab 13.

Table 13-2
Software required for Lab 13

Software	Location
Lab 13 student worksheet	Lab13_worksheet.rtf (provided by instructor)

Working with Lab Worksheets

Each lab in this manual requires that you answer questions, shoot screen shots, and perform other activities that you will document in a worksheet named for the lab, such as Lab13_worksheet.rtf. Your instructor will provide you with access to the worksheets. It is recommended that you use a USB flash drive to store your worksheets, so that you can submit them to your instructor for review. As you perform the exercises in each lab, open the appropriate worksheet file using WordPad, fill in the required information, and save the file to your flash drive.

SCENARIO

You are a Windows 7 technical specialist for Contoso, Ltd., a company with workstations in a variety of different environments. You have been assigned the task of building a test web server on the company's laboratory network. The web server must host two separate Web sites, one public site for Internet users and one intranet site for company employees.

After completing this lab, you will be able to:

- Deploy Web sites on Windows 7

- Configure Windows Firewall

- Create firewall rules

Estimated lab time: 60 minutes

Exercise 13.1	Installing Internet Information Server
Overview	Because this is only a test deployment, you will be using a Windows 7 computer to function as the web server. In Exercise 13.1, you install Internet Information Services on your workstation and configure it to host two Web sites.
Completion time	15 minutes

1. Turn on the NYC-CLa workstation and log on using the **contoso\Administrator** account and the password **Pa$$w0rd**.

2. Click Start. Then click Control Panel. The Control Panel window appears.

3. Click Programs > Programs and Features. The Uninstall or change a program window appears.

4. Click Turn Windows features on or off. The Windows Features dialog box appears.

5. Browse to the Internet Information Services\World Wide Web Services folder, as shown in Figure 13-1.

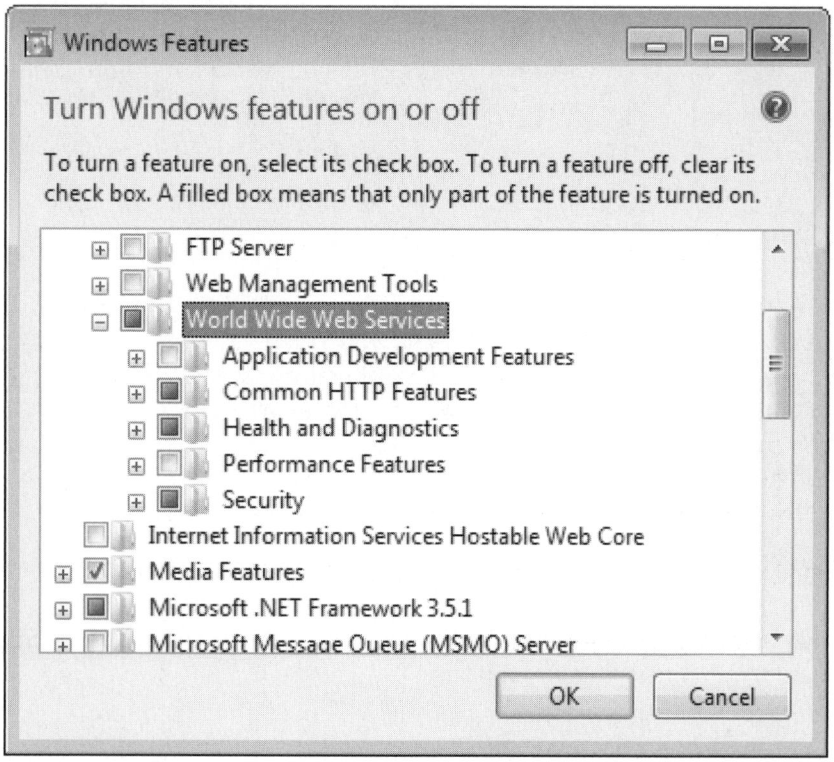

Figure 13-1
The World Wide Web Services folder in the Windows Features dialog box

6. Select the Common HTTP Features, Health and Diagnostics, and Security check boxes.

7. Expand the Web Management Tools folder and select the IIS Management Console check box. Then click OK. Windows 7 installs the selected components.

8. Close the Programs and Features control panel window.

9. Click Start, and then click Control Panel. The Control Panel window appears.

10. Click System and Security > Administrative Tools. The Administrative Tools window appears.

11. Double click Internet Information Services (IIS) Manager. The Internet Information Services (IIS) Manager console appears, as shown in Figure 13-2.

Figure 13-2
The Internet Information Services (IIS) Manager console

12. Expand the NYC-CLa container, and then expand the Sites folder.

13. Right click the Sites folder and, from the context menu, select Add Web Site. The Add Web Site dialog box appears.

14. In the Site name text box, type **Intranet**.

15. In the Physical path text box, type **c:\inetpub\wwwroot**.

16. Change the value in the Port text box to **4444**.

17. Click OK. The new intranet Web site appears in the Sites folder.

Question 1	*What URL would you use in your computer's browser to test the functionality of the intranet Web site you just created?*

18. Take a screen shot of the Internet Information Services (IIS) Manager console, showing the new site you created, by pressing Alt+Prt Scr, and then paste the resulting image into the Lab13_worksheet file in the page provided by pressing Ctrl+V.

19. Close the Internet Information Services (IIS) Manager console.

20. Leave the computer logged on for the next exercise.

Exercise 13.2	Testing IIS Connectivity
Overview	In Exercise 13.2, you test the functionality of the web server you just installed.
Completion time	20 minutes

NOTE	*In a classroom lab environment, students should work with partners so that they have access to a second workstation they can use as a test client. After one partner completes the remaining exercises in the lab, the two can swap roles, allowing the other partner to work with Windows Firewall on the other workstation.*

1. Click Start, and then click All Programs > Internet Explorer. An Internet Explorer window appears.

2. In the address box, type **http://127.0.0.1** and press Enter.

Question 2	*What is the result, and what does the result indicate?*

3. Next, test the intranet Web site by using the URL you specified in Exercise 13.1.

Question 3	*What is the result, and what does it indicate?*

4.   Using another Windows 7 workstation as your test client, log on using the **contoso\Administrator** username and the password **Pa$$w0rd**.

5.   Open Internet Explorer and attempt to access the IIS web server running on your NYC-CLa workstation by typing **http://nyc-cla** (where a is the number of your workstation) in the address box and pressing Enter.

Question 4	What is the result?

6.   Now, try to connect to the intranet Web site from the test client computer.

Question 5	What is the result?

Question 6	List three possible reasons why you might be unable to connect to your computer's web server using a browser on another computer.

7.   Back on the NYC-CLa workstation, click Start, and then click Control Panel > System and Security > Windows Firewall. The Windows Firewall control panel appears, as shown in Figure 13-3.

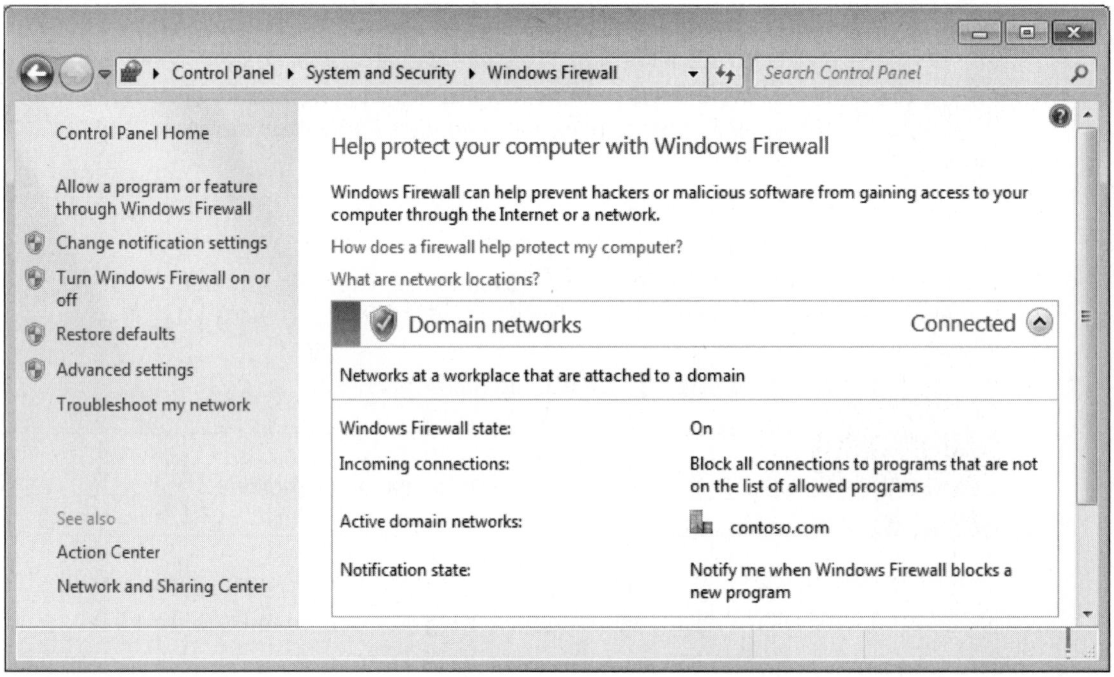

Figure 13-3
The Windows Firewall control panel

8. Click Turn Windows Firewall on or off. The *Customize settings for each type of network* window appears.

9. Under Domain network location settings, select the Turn off Windows Firewall (not recommended) option and click OK.

10. Return to your test client computer and try again to access both of the sites on the web server using Internet Explorer.

Question 7	What are the results, and what do the results indicate?

Question 8	What other test could you perform to prove that it was your computer's firewall that was blocking the connection and not the firewall on the computer you are using as a client?

11. Clear the Internet Explorer cache on the test client computer by clicking Tools > Internet Options. The Internet Options dialog box appears.

12. Under Browsing History, click the Delete button. The Delete Browsing History dialog box appears.

13. Click Delete. Then click OK to close the Internet Options dialog box.

Question 9	Why is it necessary to clear the cache before you retest the web server connections?

14. Back on your NYC-CLa workstation computer in the Windows Firewall control panel, open the *Customize settings for each type of network* window again.

15. Under Domain network location settings, select the Turn on Windows Firewall option and click OK.

Question 10	Why can you not simply leave Windows Firewall turned off when you deploy an actual web server?

16. Leave the Windows Firewall control panel open and the workstations logged on for the next exercise.

Exercise 13.3	Allowing a Program through the Firewall
Overview	Windows Firewall is preventing clients from connecting to the web server. In Exercise 13.3, to enable client access, you will use the Windows Firewall control panel to allow access to the web server.
Completion time	10 minutes

1. On your NYC-CLa workstation, in the Windows Firewall control panel, click Allow a program or feature through Windows Firewall. The *Allow programs to communicate through Windows Firewall* window appears, as shown in Figure 13-4.

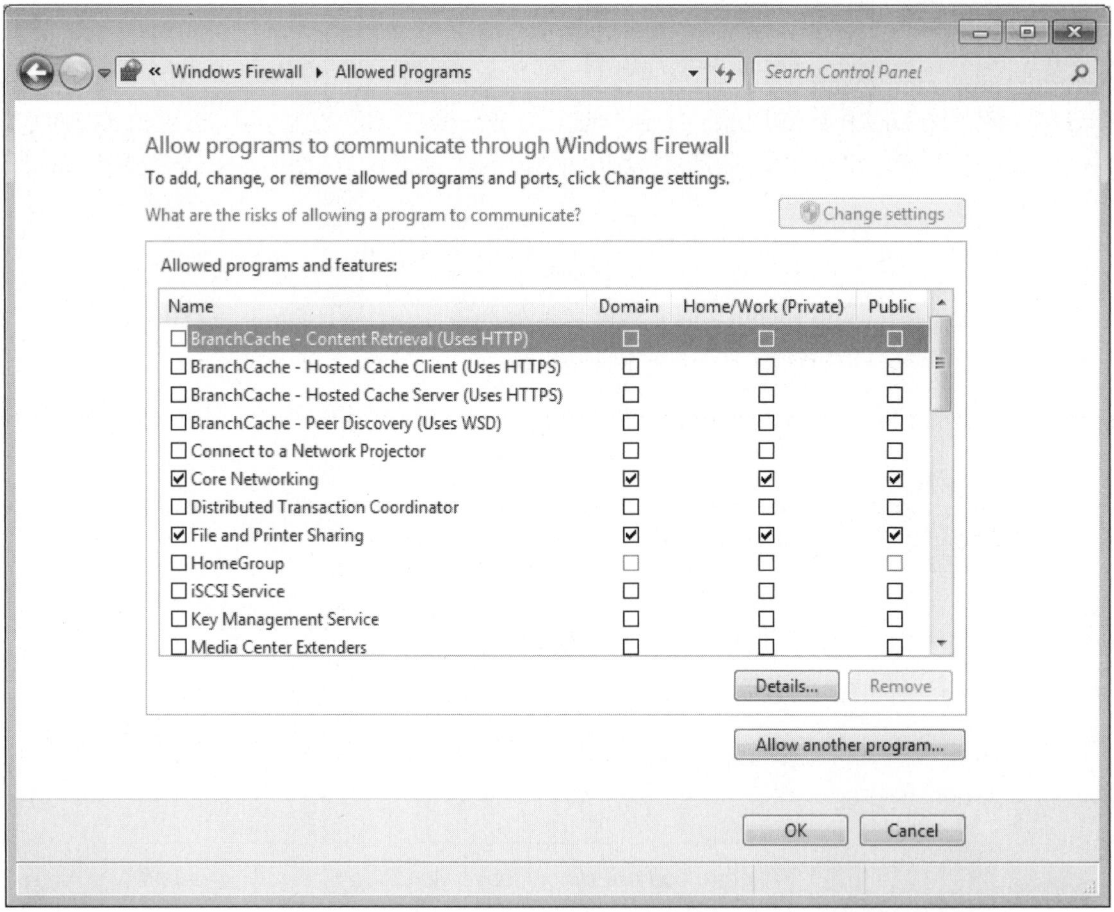

Figure 13-4
The *Allow programs to communicate through Windows Firewall* window

2. Scroll down in the *Allowed programs and features* list, select the World Wide Web Services (HTTP) check box, and click OK.

3. Return to your test client computer and try again to connect to the default Web site at **http://nyc-cla**.

Question 11	*Why are you now able to connect to the Web site from the client?*

4.   Now test the connection to the intranet Web site.

Question 12	*Why are you unable to connect to the intranet site from the client?*

5.   Open the *Allow programs to communicate through Windows Firewall* window again and clear the World Wide Web Services (HTTP) check box. Then, click OK.

6.   Leave the remaining windows open and the workstations logged on for the next exercise.

Exercise 13.4	Creating Windows Firewall Rules
Overview	The port you opened in Exercise 13.3 enables clients to access the default Web site hosted by your web server, but not the intranet Web site. In this exercise, you use the Windows Firewall with Advanced Security console to create rules that will enable clients to access both Web sites.
Completion time	15 minutes

1.   On your NYC-CLa workstation, click Start. Then click Control Panel > System and Security > Administrative Tools. The Administrative Tools window appears.

2.   Double click Windows Firewall with Advanced Security. The Windows Firewall with Advanced Security console appears, as shown in Figure 13-5.

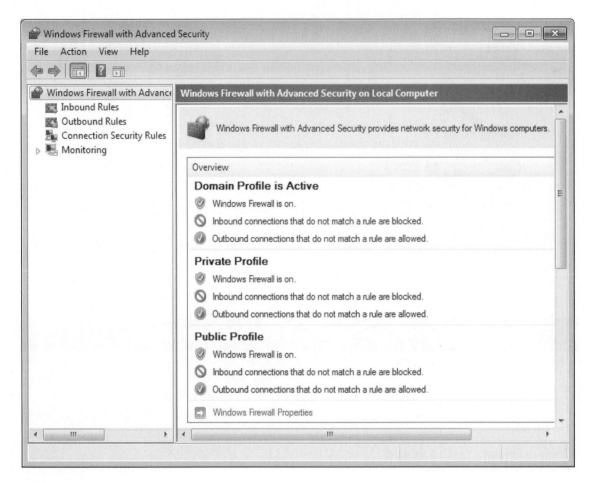

Figure 13-5
The Windows Firewall with Advanced Security console

3. Select the Inbound Rules container. The list of default inbound rules appears.

4. Scroll down to the bottom of the list and locate the rules for World Wide Web Services (HTTP Traffic-In).

Question 13	Why are there two separate rules for the World Wide Web Services?

5. Double click each of the two rules and examine their properties.

Question 14	How do the properties of the two rules differ?

Question 15	How would the opening of the port you performed in Exercise 13.3 affect the World Wide Web Services (HTTP Traffic-In) rules you just examined?

6. Select the Inbound Rules container and, from the Action menu, select Filter By Profile > Filter By Domain Profile.

Question 16	*What happens to the list of rules?*

7. Right click the Inbound Rules container and, from the context menu, select New Rule. The New Inbound Rule Wizard launches, displaying the *Rule Type* page, as shown in Figure 13-6.

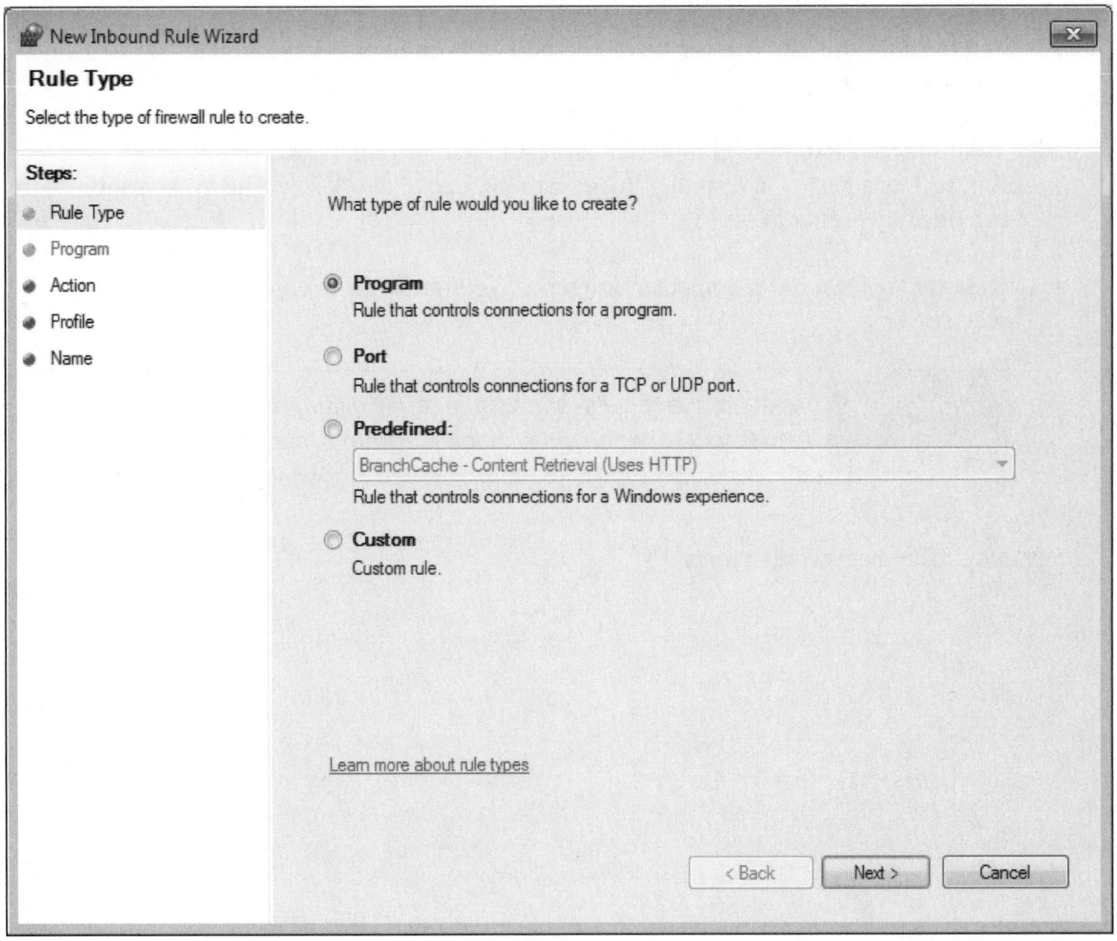

Figure 13-6
Rule Type page

8. Select the Port option and click Next. The *Protocol and Ports* page appears.

9. Leave the default TCP and Specific local ports options selected. In the *Specific local ports* text box, type **80, 4444** and click Next. The *Action* page appears.

10. Leave the default *Allow the connection* option selected and click Next. The *Profile* page appears.

11. Clear the Private and Public check boxes, leaving only the Domain check box selected, and then click Next. The *Name* page appears.

12. In the Name text box, type **Lab Web Server—Ports 80 & 4444** and click Finish. The wizard creates and enables the new rule and then adds it to the Inbound Rules list.

 *How would the rule creation procedure you just performed differ if you wanted to restrict client access to the intranet Web site to computers on the local network only?*

13. Double click the rule you just created. The Lab Web Server—Ports 80 & 4444 Properties sheet appears.

14. Take a screen shot of the Properties sheet for the new rule by pressing Alt+Prt Scr, and then paste the resulting image into the Lab13_worksheet file in the page provided by pressing Ctrl+V.

15. Return to the test client computer and repeat your attempts to connect to both web servers.

Question 18 *What are the results, and why are they different from the results you experienced with the program exception?*

16. Log off of both workstations.

LAB 14
REMOTE WINDOWS 7 ADMINISTRATION

This lab contains the following exercises and activities:

Exercise 14.1   Creating a Custom MMC Console

Exercise 14.2   Configuring Remote Desktop Access

Exercise 14.3   Connecting to a Remote Workstation

Exercise 14.4   Creating an RDP File

Lab Challenge 14.1   Using Windows Remote Management

BEFORE YOU BEGIN

The lab environment consists of student workstations connected to a local area network, along with a server that functions as the domain controller for a domain called contoso.com. The computers required for this lab are listed in Table 14-1.

Table 14-1
Computers required for Lab 14

Computer	Operating System	Computer Name
Server	Windows Server 2008 R2	RWDC01
Workstation 1	Windows 7 Enterprise	NYC-CLa
Workstation 2	Windows 7 Enterprise	NYC-CLb

In a classroom lab environment, there will be one classroom server and the students will have workstations named using consecutive numbers in place of the a and b variables. In a virtual lab environment, each student will have three virtual machines, named RWDC01, NYC-CL1, and NYC-CL2.

In addition to the computers, you will also require the software listed in Table 14-2 to complete Lab 14.

Table 14-2
Software required for Lab 14

Software	Location
Lab 14 student worksheet	Lab14_worksheet.rtf (provided by instructor)

Working with Lab Worksheets

Each lab in this manual requires that you answer questions, shoot screen shots, and perform other activities that you will document in a worksheet named for the lab, such as Lab14_worksheet.rtf. Your instructor will provide you with access to the worksheets. It is recommended that you use a USB flash drive to store your worksheets, so that you can submit them to your instructor for review. As you perform the exercises in each lab, open the appropriate worksheet file using WordPad, fill in the required information, and save the file to your flash drive.

SCENARIO

You are a newly hired desktop technician for Contoso, Ltd., working on a long-term test deployment of new Windows 7 workstations. You have been given the task of testing the various remote administration technologies included with Windows 7.

After completing this lab, you will be able to:

- Create a custom MMC console

- Configure the Windows 7 Remote Access technologies

- Use Remote Desktop to connect to an unattended computer

- Create an RDP file

Estimated lab time: 60 minutes

Exercise 14.1   Creating a Custom MMC Console

Overview	Rather than evaluate the system events on each workstation individually, you can create a customized Microsoft Management Console interface containing the Event Viewer snap-in for multiple computers.
Completion time	20 minutes

> **NOTE**
> In a classroom lab environment, students should work with partners so that they have access to a second workstation. After one partner completes each exercise, the two can swap roles, allowing the other partner to complete the exercise as well.

1. Turn on the NYC-CLa workstation and log on using the **contoso\Administrator** account and the password **Pa$$w0rd**.

2. Click Start. Then, in the Search programs and files box, type **mmc** and press Enter. A blank MMC console appears, as shown in Figure 14-1.

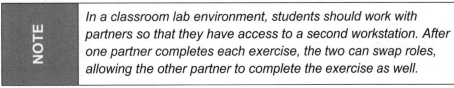

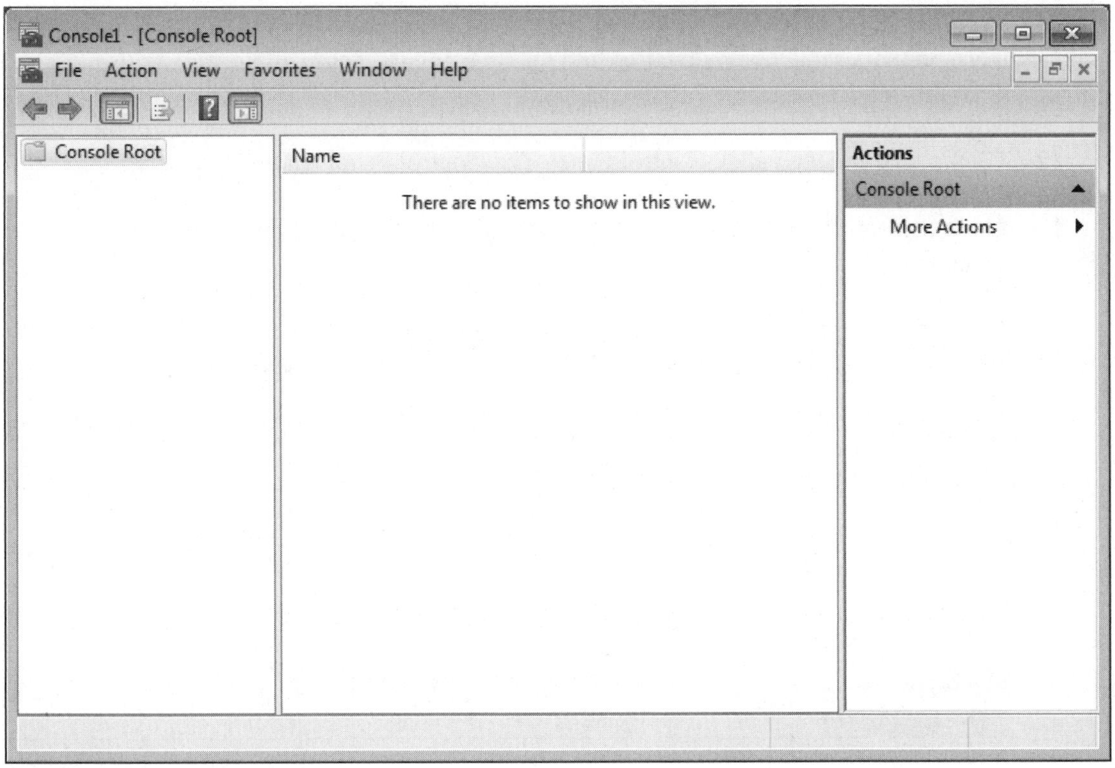

Figure 14-1
A blank MMC console

3. Click File > Add/Remove Snap-in. The Add or Remove Snap-ins dialog box appears.

4. In the Available snap-ins list, select Event Viewer and click Add. The Select Computer dialog box appears.

5. Leave the Local computer option selected and click OK. The Event Viewer (Local) snap-in appears in the Selected snap-ins list.

6. In the Available snap-ins list, select Event Viewer again and click Add. The Select Computer dialog box appears again.

7. Select the Another computer option and click Browse. Another Select Computer dialog box appears.

8. In the Enter the object name to select box, type **nyc-clb**, where b is the number of your partner's computer, and click OK. The computer name appears in the first Select Computer dialog box.

9. Click OK. An Event Viewer message box appears, stating that Event Viewer cannot connect to your partner computer because the RPC server is not available.

10. Click OK to close the message box.

11. Turn on the NYC-CLb workstation and log on using the **contoso\Administrator** account and the password **Pa$$w0rd**.

12. Click Start, and then click Control Panel. The Control Panel window appears.

13. Click System and Security > Windows Firewall. The Windows Firewall control panel appears.

14. Click Allow a program or feature through Windows Firewall. The *Allow programs to communicate through Windows Firewall* window appears.

15. Scroll down in the Allowed programs and features list, select the Remote Event Log Management check box, and then click OK.

16. Back on workstation NYC-CLa, repeat steps 6 to 8 to add the Event Viewer snap-in for workstation NYC-CLb again.

Question 1	*How can you find out which port Windows Firewall opened up on NYC-CLb?* Inbound Rules

17. Click OK. The Event Viewer (NYC-CLb.contoso.com) snap-in appears in the Selected snap-ins list.

18. Take a screen shot of the Add or Remove Snap-ins dialog box, showing the two Event Viewer instances you added, by pressing Alt+Prt Scr, and then paste the resulting image into the Lab14_worksheet file in the page provided by pressing Ctrl+V.

19. Click OK. The snap-ins appear in the MMC console.

20. Click File > Exit. A Microsoft Management Console message box appears, prompting you to save the console settings.

21. Click Yes. A Save As combo box appears.

22. Click Save.

23. Leave the workstation logged on for the next exercise.

Exercise 14.2	Configuring Remote Desktop Access
Overview	Before you can test the Remote Desktop program, both of the Windows 7 computers involved must be configured to allow secured connections to occur. In Exercise 14.2, both you and your partner configure the Remote Access settings on your individual computers.
Completion time	5 minutes

1. Click Start, and then click Control Panel. The Control Panel window appears.

2. Click System and Security > System. The System control panel appears.

3. Click Remote Settings. The System Properties sheet appears with the Remote tab selected, as shown in Figure 14-2.

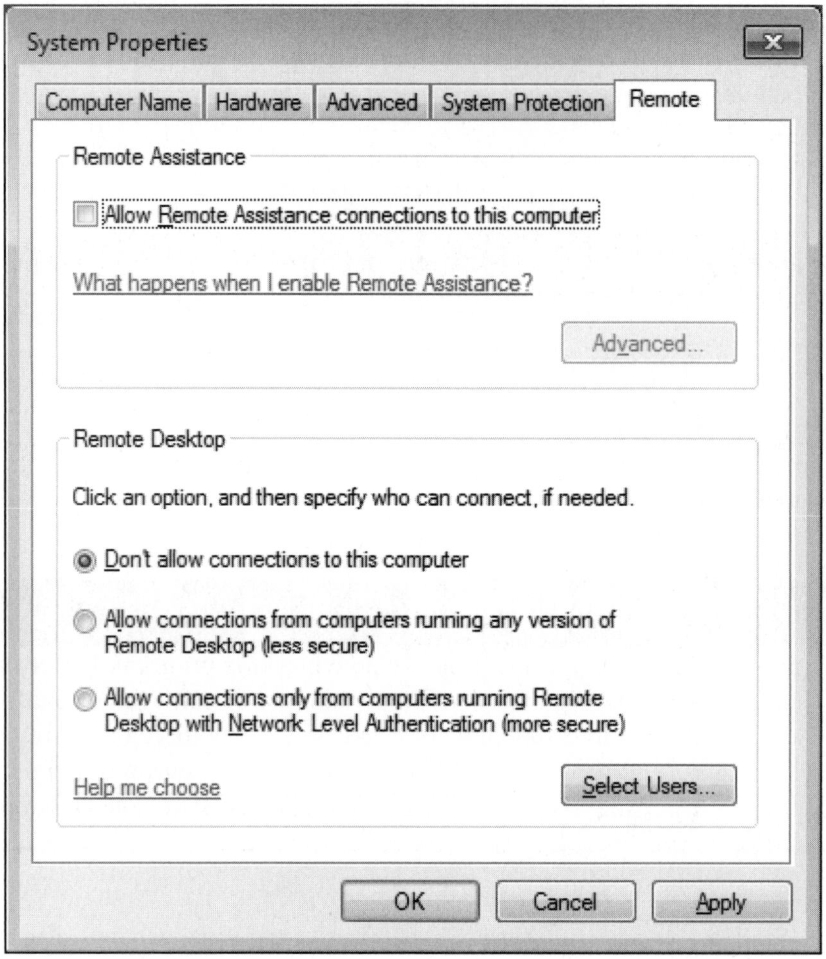

Figure 14-2
The System Properties sheet

4. Select the Allow Remote Assistance connections to this computer check box and, in the Remote Desktop box, select the *Allow connections from computers running any version of Remote Desktop* option and click Advanced. The Remote Assistance Settings dialog box appears.

5. Make sure that the Allow this computer to be controlled remotely check box is selected. In the Invitations box, set the maximum amount of time that invitations can remain open to 24 Hours and click OK.

Question 2	When using Remote Assistance, why might it be necessary to impose a time limit on the invitation? *So They cannot log into your computer any Time They want.*

6. Click OK to close the System Properties dialog box.

7. Leave the computer logged on for the next exercise.

Repeat Exercise 14.2 on the NYC-CLb workstation, so that both computers can support Remote Desktop connections.

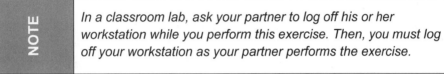

Exercise 14.3	Connecting to a Remote Workstation
Overview	The Remote Desktop feature in Windows 7 does not require a user to be present at the remote computer. In Exercise 14.3, you and your partner take turns connecting to each others' computers and controlling them from a remote location.
Completion time	15 minutes

In a classroom lab, ask your partner to log off his or her workstation while you perform this exercise. Then, you must log off your workstation as your partner performs the exercise.

1. Click Start. Point to All Programs > Accessories, and click Remote Desktop Connection. The Remote Desktop Connection window appears.

2. Click Options. The *Remote Desktop Connection* window expands, as shown in Figure 14-3.

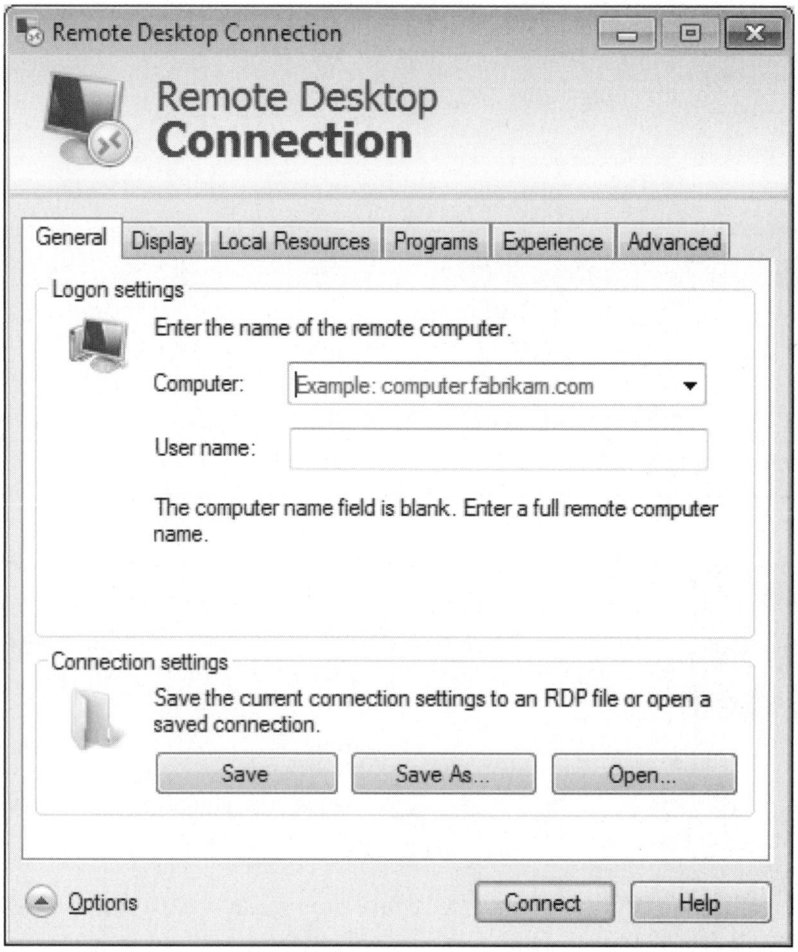

Figure 14-3
The expanded *Remote Desktop Connection* window

3. On the General tab in the Computer text box, type **NYC-CLb**, where b is the number of your partner's computer.

4. Click the Display tab.

5. Set the Display Configuration slider to 800 by 600 pixels.

6. Click the Local Resources tab.

7. Clear the Printers check box and click the More button. The Local devices and resources dialog box appears.

8. Select the Drives check box, and click OK.

9. Click the Experience tab.

10. From the Choose your connection speed to optimize performance drop-down list, select LAN (10 Mbps or Higher).

11. Click Connect. A Remote Desktop Connection message box appears, prompting you to confirm that you trust the remote computer.

12. Select the Don't ask me again for connections to this computer check box and click Connect.

13. Type the password **Pa$$w0rd** for the contoso\Administrator account and click OK.

14. A NYC-CLb Remote Desktop Connection window appears, containing an image of the remote computer's desktop.

15. Take a screen shot of the NYC-CLb Remote Desktop Connection window by pressing Alt+Prt Scr, and then paste the resulting image into the Lab14_worksheet file in the page provided by pressing Ctrl+V.

16. NYC-CLb Remote Desktop Connection window, click Start. Then click All Programs > Accessories > Notepad. A Notepad window appears.

Question 3	On which computer is the Notepad program actually running? *On brittons computer*

17. In the Notepad window, click File > Open. The Open combo box appears.

Question 4	When you browse the Local Disk (C:) drive in the Open combo box, which computer's C: drive are you actually looking at? *brittons*

18. In the Open combo box, select the Computer container, and scroll down to display the NYC-CLa disks under Other.

19. Take a screen shot of the NYC-CLb Remote Desktop Connection window, showing the NYC-CLa disks in the Open combo box, by pressing Alt+Prt Scr, and then paste the resulting image into the Lab14_worksheet file in the page provided by pressing Ctrl+V.

Question 5	Why Is it possible to access the host computer's—that is, the NYC-CLa computer's—various drives while working in the NYC-CLb Remote Desktop Connection window? *because to click box to access the drives*

20. Click Cancel to close the Open combo box.

Question 6	During a Remote Desktop session, what would happen if you opened the Network Connections window on the remote computer and configured the network adapter to use a different IP address? Explain the result. *Would not be able to connect*

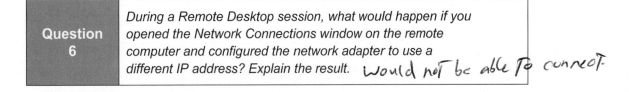

21. Close the Notepad window.

22. Close the *NYC-CLb Remote Desktop Connection* window. A Remote Desktop Connection message box appears, informing you that this will disconnect the Remote Desktop session.

23. Click OK. The *NYC-CLb Remote Desktop Connection* window closes.

24. Leave the workstation logged on for the next exercise.

Exercise 14.4	Creating an RDP File
Overview	The Remote Desktop feature in Windows 7 does not require a user to be present at the remote computer. In Exercise 14.4, you and your partner take turns connecting to each others' computers and controlling them from a remote location.
Completion time	10 minutes

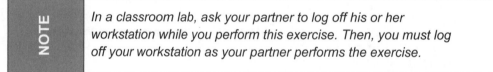

> **NOTE** *In a classroom lab, ask your partner to log off his or her workstation while you perform this exercise. Then, you must log off your workstation as your partner performs the exercise.*

1. Click Start. Point to All Programs > Accessories, and click Remote Desktop Connection. The *Remote Desktop Connection* window appears.

2. Click Options. The *Remote Desktop Connection* window expands.

3. On the General tab in the Computer text box, type **NYC-CLb**, where b is the number of your partner's computer.

4. In the User name text box, if it does not appear there already, type **contoso\Administrator**.

5. Click the Display tab.

6. Set the Display Configuration slider to 640 by 480 pixels.

7. Click the Local Resources tab.

8. Click the More button. The *Local devices and resources* dialog box appears.

9. Clear the Drives check box, and click OK.

10. Click the Programs tab.

11. Select the *Start the following program on connection* check box.

12. In the Program path and file name, type **c:\windows\notepad.exe**.

13. Click the General tab, and then click Save As. The Save As combo box appears.

14. Under Favorites, select the Desktop container.

15. In the File name text box, type **NYC-CLb RDC** and click Save. An NYC-CLb RDC icon appears on the desktop.

16. Close the Remote Desktop Connection window.

17. Take a screen shot of the desktop, showing the NYC-CLb RDC icon, by pressing Prt Scr, and then paste the resulting image into the Lab14_worksheet file in the page provided by pressing Ctrl+V.

18. Double click the NYC-CLb RDC icon. The Windows Security dialog box appears.

19. Type the password **Pa$$w0rd** for the contoso\Administrator user. Then click OK. The *NYC-CLb RDC Remote Desktop Connection* window appears.

Question 7	Why doesn't the Notepad.exe program open in the Remote Desktop Connection *window, despite your having configured it in the RDP file?* *The Identity cannot be verified*

20. Close the *NYC-CLb RDC Remote Desktop Connection* window and click OK to disconnect the session.

21. Log off of the workstation.

LAB CHALLENGE 14.1: USING WINDOWS REMOTE MANAGEMENT

Completion time	10 minutes

Windows Remote Management is a service that enables administrators to execute command line programs on a remote computer by running a remote shell program called Winrs.exe. To complete this challenge, you must write out the complete procedure for enabling Windows Remote Management and executing a command that uses the contoso\Administrator account to create a local user account for a user called Mark Lee (**MLee**) with the password **Pa$$w0rd** on the remote workstation. After writing out the procedure, execute it on your workstation (in cooperation with your partner) and take a screen shot showing the creation of the user account.

LAB 15
ADMINISTERING WINDOWS 7

This lab contains the following exercises and activities:

Exercise 15.1   Creating a Custom Backup Job

Exercise 15.2   Performing an Incremental Backup

Exercise 15.3   Performing a Restore

Lab Challenge 15.1   Scheduling a Backup Job

Lab Challenge 15.2   Using BranchCache

BEFORE YOU BEGIN

The lab environment consists of student workstations connected to a local area network, along with a server that functions as the domain controller for a domain called contoso.com. The computers required for this lab are listed in Table 15-1.

Table 15-1
Computers required for Lab 15

Computer	Operating System	Computer Name
Server	Windows Server 2008 R2	RWDC01
Workstation 1	Windows 7 Enterprise	NYC-CLa

In a classroom lab environment, there will be one classroom server and the students will have workstations named using consecutive numbers in place of the a and b variables. In a virtual lab environment, each student will have three virtual machines, named RWDC01, NYC-CL1, and NYC-CL2.

In addition to the computers, you will also require the software listed in Table 15-2 to complete Lab 15.

Table 15-2
Software required for Lab 15

Software	Location
Remote Server Administration Tools for Windows 7	Installed in Lab 10
Lab 15 student worksheet	Lab15_worksheet.rtf (provided by instructor)

Working with Lab Worksheets

Each lab in this manual requires that you answer questions, shoot screen shots, and perform other activities that you will document in a worksheet named for the lab, such as Lab15_worksheet.rtf. Your instructor will provide you with access to the worksheets. It is recommended that you use a USB flash drive to store your worksheets, so that you can submit them to your instructor for review. As you perform the exercises in each lab, open the appropriate worksheet file using WordPad, fill in the required information, and save the file to your flash drive.

SCENARIO

Alice, the user from Lab 6, calls to report that her data files are not being backed up in any way, and that someone told her this was bad. After explaining the need for regular backups to her, you demonstrate the process of creating a single backup job, and then configure her computer to perform weekly backups of her data files and her entire system drive.

After completing this lab, you will be able to:

- Create a single backup job

- Understand incremental backups

- Restore files from a backup

- Schedule a backup job

Estimated lab time: 70 minutes

Exercise 15.1 Creating a Custom Backup Job

Overview	In Exercise 15.1, you create a single, custom backup job that saves selected files and folders to a partition on the computer's hard disk.
Completion time	20 minutes

In a classroom lab environment, it is assumed that you have completed Lab 6, and that your hard disk has an X: drive with the partition name Alice1. If this is not the case, please complete Lab 6 before proceeding.

1. Turn on the NYC-CLa workstation and log on using the **contoso\Administrator** account and the password **Pa$$w0rd**.

2. Click Start. Then, click Control Panel. The Control Panel window appears.

3. Click System and Security > Backup and Restore. The Backup and Restore control panel appears.

4. Click Set up backup. The Set Up Backup Wizard appears, displaying the *Select where you want to save your backup* page, as shown in Figure 15-1.

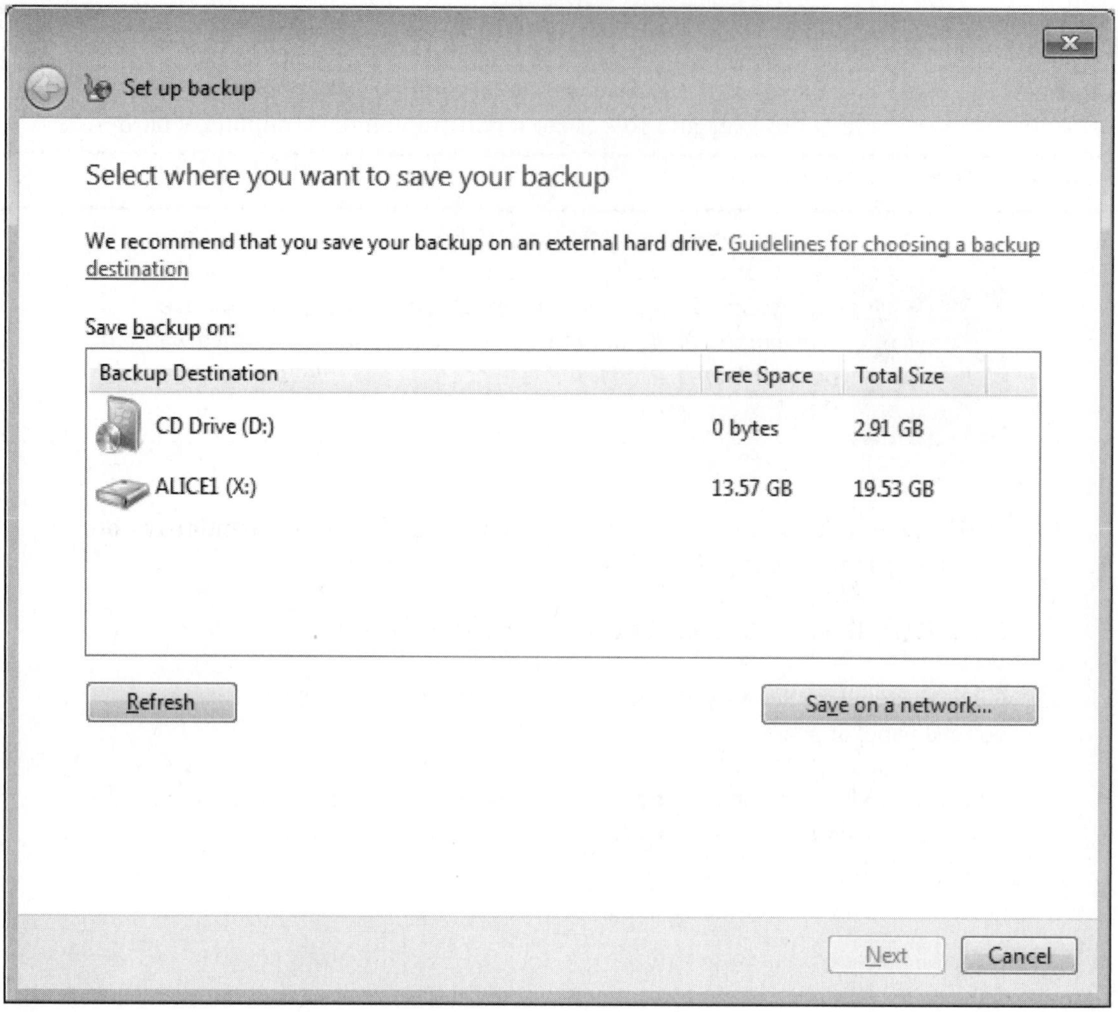

Figure 15-1
The *Select where you want to save your backup* page

5.   Select the ALICE1 (X:) partition and click Next. The *What do you want to back up?* page appears.

Question 1	Why doesn't the system drive (C:) appear on the *Select where you want to save your backup* page? *drive (c:) is The VM computer Hard drive which is To be backed up.*

Question 2	Why does a warning appear when you select the ALICE1 (X:) drive, informing you that the X: drive is on the same physical disk as your system drive?

6.   Select the Let me choose option and click Next. The *What do you want to back up?* page appears.

7.   Expand the Local Disk (C:) container.

Question 3	*Why doesn't the Windows folder appear under the Local Disk (C:) drive?*

8.   Select the Local Disk (C:) check box and clear the Include a system image of drives: System Reserved, (C:) check box. Then click Next. The *Review your backup settings* page appears.

9.   Click Change Schedule. The *How often do you want to back up?* page appears.

10. Clear the Run backup on a schedule (recommended) check box and click OK. The schedule indicator on the *Review your backup settings* page changes to *On demand*.

11. Take a screen shot of the *Review your backup settings* page by pressing Alt+Prt Scr, and then paste the resulting image into the Lab15_worksheet file in the page provided by pressing Ctrl+V.

12. Click Save settings and run backup. The Backup and Restore control panel now shows the backup in progress.

13. Click View Details. A Windows Backup is currently in progress window appears, displaying the names of the files the program is copying.

NOTE	*The backup process can take several minutes.*

14. Take a screen shot of the *Windows Backup is currently in progress* page by pressing Alt+Prt Scr, and then paste the resulting image into the Lab15_worksheet file in the page provided by pressing Ctrl+V.

15. Click Close.

Question 4	*What is the size of the backup, as indicated on the Backup and Restore control panel?*

16. Close the Backup and Restore control panel.

17. Leave the computer logged on for the next exercise.

Exercise 15.2	Performing an Incremental Backup
Overview	In Exercise 15.2, you create a new file on the computer and repeat the backup job you performed in Exercise 15.1, to demonstrate how incremental backup jobs work in Windows 7.
Completion time	15 minutes

1. Click Start. Then click All Programs > Accessories > Notepad. The Notepad window appears.

2. Type some text in the Notepad window, and then click File > Save As. The Save As combo box appears.

3. In the File name text box, type **c:\newfile.txt** and click Save. Notepad creates the new file at the root of the C: drive.

4. Open the Backup and Restore control panel, just as you did in Exercise 15.1.

Question 5	How is the Backup and Restore control panel interface different from when you opened it the first time?

5. Click Back up now. The program repeats the backup job you configured earlier.

Question 6	How does the time required for this backup compare with that for the same job the first time you ran it?

6. Switch to the Notepad window.

7. Modify the text you typed in the Notepad window and click File > Save.

8. Switch back to the Backup and Restore control panel and click Back up now again. The program performs a third backup.

9. Click Start. Then click All Programs > Accessories > Windows Explorer. The Windows Explorer window appears.

10. Browse to the ALICE1 (X:) drive, expand the NYC-CLa container, and select the folder beginning with Backup Set.

Question 7	*How many Backup Files folders are there beneath the Backup Set folder?*

11. Take a screen shot of the Windows Explorer window, showing the Backup Files folders, by pressing Alt+Prt Scr, and then paste the resulting image into the Lab15_worksheet file in the page provided by pressing Ctrl+V.

12. Right click the Backup Files folder with the earliest timestamp and, from the context menu, select Properties. The Properties sheet for the folder appears.

Question 8	*What is the size of the folder?*

13. Click OK to close the Properties sheet.

14. Open the Properties sheet for the second Backup Files folder.

Question 9	*Why is the second Backup Files folder so much smaller than the first one?*

15. Click OK to close the Properties sheet.

16. Leave the workstation logged on for the next exercise.

Exercise 15.3	Performing a Restore
Overview	The only way to be sure that a backup has completed successfully is to perform a test restore. In this exercise, you restore a file from the backup you performed earlier.
Completion time	10 minutes

1. In the Backup and Restore control panel, scroll down to the Restore area, as shown in Figure 15-2.

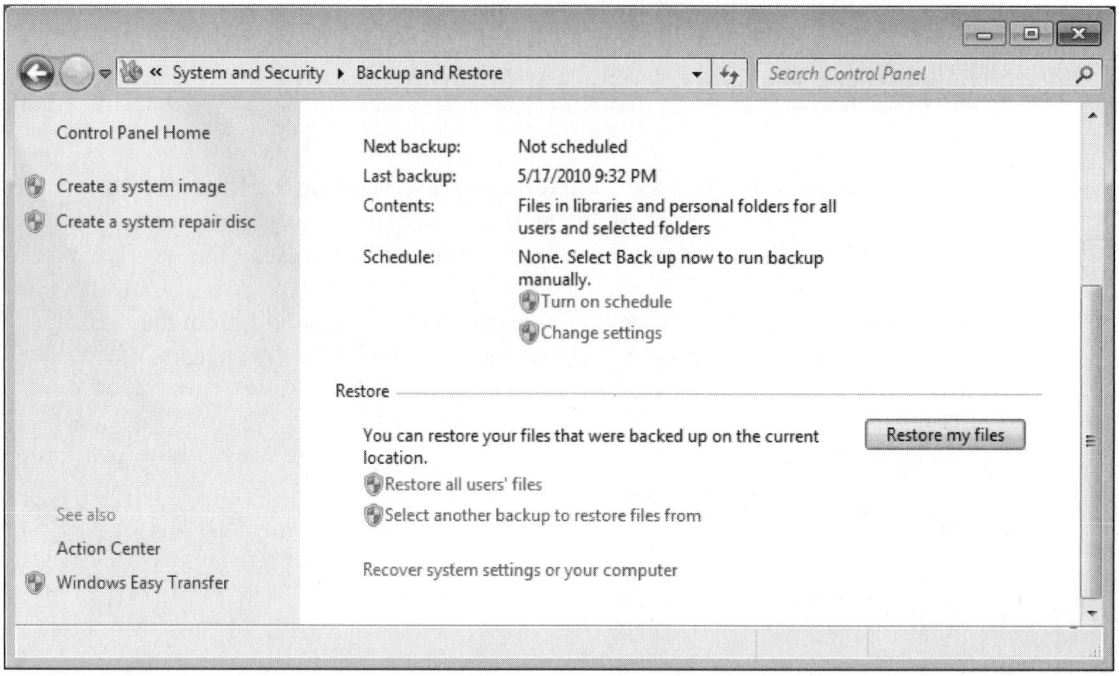

Figure 15-2
The Restore area of the Backup and Restore control panel

2.   Click Restore my files. The Restore Files Wizard appears, displaying the *Browse or search your backup for files and folders to restore* page.

3.   Click Choose a different date. The Restore Files dialog box appears.

Question 10	How many options are there to choose from in the Restore Files dialog box?

4.   Click Cancel. The Restore Files dialog box closes.

5.   Click Search. The Search for files to restore dialog box appears.

6.   In the Search for text box, type **newfile.txt** and click Search.

Question 11	How many results appear in the Search for files to restore dialog box and from which backup jobs are they?

7.   Click Select all, and then click OK. Newfile.txt appears on the *Browse or search your backup for files and folders to restore* page.

Question 12	*From which of the three backups you performed is the Newfile.txt file going to be restored?*

8. Click Next. The *Where do you want to restore your files?* page appears.

9. Select the *In the following location* option and, in the text box, type **x:** and click Restore. The wizard performs the restore and the *Your files have been restored* page appears.

10. Take a screen shot of the *Your files have been restored* page by pressing Alt+Prt Scr, and then paste the resulting image into the Lab15_worksheet file in the page provided by pressing Ctrl+V.

11. Click Finish.

12. Close the Backup and Restore control panel and log off of the workstation.

LAB CHALLENGE 15.1: SCHEDULING A BACKUP JOB

Completion time	10 minutes

Performing a single backup job provides only limited protection against hardware failure. To fully protect your data, you must back up regularly, and Windows 7 enables you to schedule backup jobs to run at specified intervals. To complete this challenge, you must create a job that backs up your workstation's entire system (C:) drive to the X: drive every Friday at 11:00 PM. Write out the procedure for creating the job and take a screen shot of the *Review your backup settings* page by pressing Alt+Prt Scr, and then paste the resulting image into the Lab15_worksheet file in the page provided by pressing Ctrl+V.

LAB CHALLENGE 15.2: USING BRANCHCACHE

Completion time	15 minutes

NOTE	*If you have not done so already, you must complete Exercise 10.1, in which you install Remote Server Administration Tools for Windows 7 and enable the Group Policy Management Tools, before you attempt to complete this challenge.*

To use BranchCache, you must configure the appropriate Group Policy settings on both the host servers and the branch office computers. To complete this challenge, you must create three Group Policy objects called **BranchCache Content Servers**, **BranchCache Hosted Cache Servers**, and **BranchCache Clients**, and configure each GPO with the settings needed to create a BranchCache implementation that uses your classroom server (RWDC01) as a hosted cache server. Write out the procedure for creating the GPOs and take screen shots of the three GPOs in the Group Policy Management Editor console by pressing Alt+Prt Scr, and then paste the resulting image into the Lab15_worksheet file in the page provided by pressing Ctrl+V.

LAB 16
CONFIGURING MOBILE OPTIONS

This lab contains the following exercises and activities:

Exercise 16.1   Configuring Power Options

Exercise 16.2   Creating a Custom Power Plan

Exercise 16.3   Using Powercfg.exe

Exercise 16.4   Using BitLocker

BEFORE YOU BEGIN

The lab environment consists of student workstations connected to a local area network, along with a server that functions as the domain controller for a domain called contoso.com. The computers required for this lab are listed in Table 16-1.

Table 16-1
Computers required for Lab 16

Computer	Operating System	Computer Name
Server	Windows Server 2008 R2	RWDC01
Workstation 1	Windows 7 Enterprise	NYC-CLa
Workstation 2	Windows 7 Enterprise	NYC-CLb

NOTE

In a classroom lab environment, there will be one classroom server and the students will have workstations named using consecutive numbers in place of the a and b variables. In a virtual lab environment, each student will have three virtual machines, named RWDC01, NYC-CL1, and NYC-CL2.

In addition to the computers, you will also require the software listed in Table 16-2 to complete Lab 16.

Table 16-2
Software required for Lab 16

Software	Location
Lab 16 student worksheet	Lab16_worksheet.rtf (provided by instructor)

NOTE

To complete Exercise 16.4, the students must have access to a workstation with an external hard drive or USB flash drive.

Working with Lab Worksheets

Each lab in this manual requires that you answer questions, shoot screen shots, and perform other activities that you will document in a worksheet named for the lab, such as Lab16_worksheet.rtf. Your instructor will provide you with access to the worksheets. It is recommended that you use a USB flash drive to store your worksheets, so that you can submit them to your instructor for review. As you perform the exercises in each lab, open the appropriate worksheet file using WordPad, fill in the required information, and save the file to your flash drive.

SCENARIO

You are a Windows 7 technical specialist for Contoso, Ltd., who has been given the task of optimizing battery life on the company's fleet of mobile computers. At the same time, your IT director believes that you should also be able to further the company's "green" initiative by coming up with power utilization settings that maximize the efficiency of the firm's Windows 7 desktops.

After completing this lab, you will be able to:

- Configure Windows 7 power options

- Create a custom power plan

- Import and export power settings using Powercfg.exe

- Configure BitLocker

Estimated lab time: 60 minutes

Exercise 16.1	Configuring Power Options
Overview	In Exercise 16.1, you examine the power settings used in the default power plans provided in Windows 7.
Completion time	20 minutes

1. Turn on the NYC-CLa workstation and log on using the **contoso\Administrator** account and the password **Pa$$w0rd**.

2. Click Start. Then, click Control Panel. The Control Panel window appears.

3. Click Hardware and Sound > Power Options. The Power Options control panel appears, as shown in Figure 16-1.

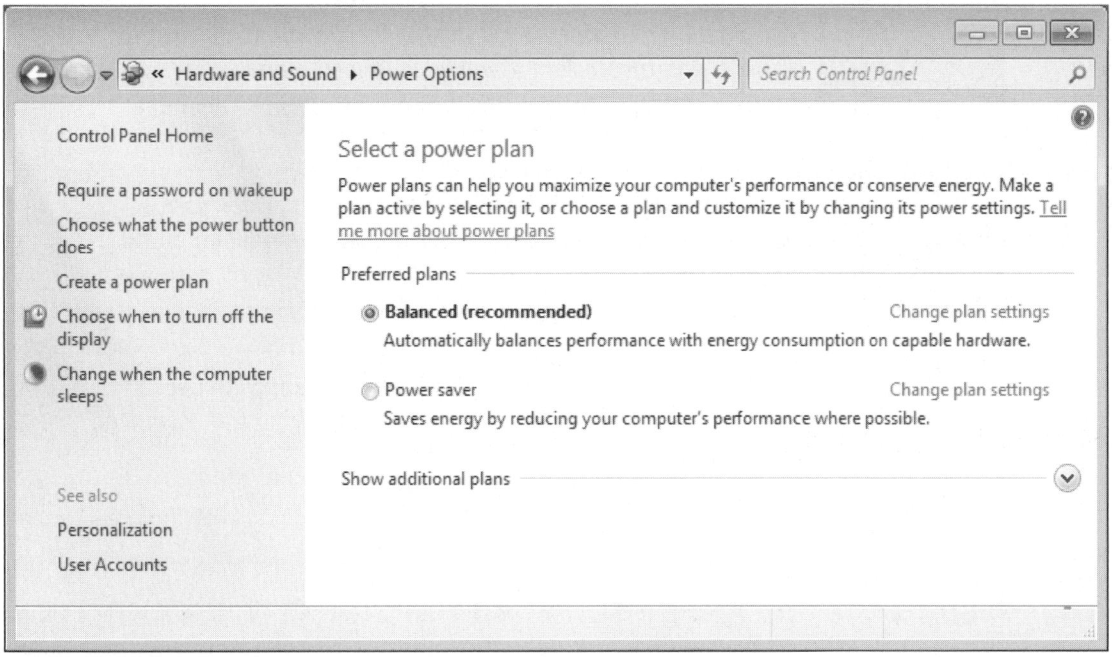

Figure 16-1
The Power Options control panel

4. Click the Show additional plans down arrow.

Question 1	How many power plans are available for your selection in the Power Options control panel?

5.   Click the Change plan settings link for the Balanced plan. The *Change settings for the plan: Balanced* page appears.

6.   Enter the values for the Turn off the display and Put the computer to sleep settings into the appropriate cells of Table 16-3.

7.   Click the Change plan settings links for the Power saver and High performance plans and enter the values for the Turn off the display and Put the computer to sleep settings into the appropriate cells of Table 16-3.

Table 16-3
Default Windows 7 power configuration settings

Setting	Balanced	Power Saver	High Performance
Turn off the display			
Put the computer to sleep			

Question 2	How do the different settings enable the Power saver plan to be more energy efficient than the Balanced plan?

Question 3	How do the different settings enable the High performance plan to achieve greater performance levels than either of the other two plans?

8.   In any one of the *Change settings for the plan* pages, click Change advanced power settings. The Power Options dialog box appears, displaying the Advanced Settings tab, as shown in Figure 16-2.

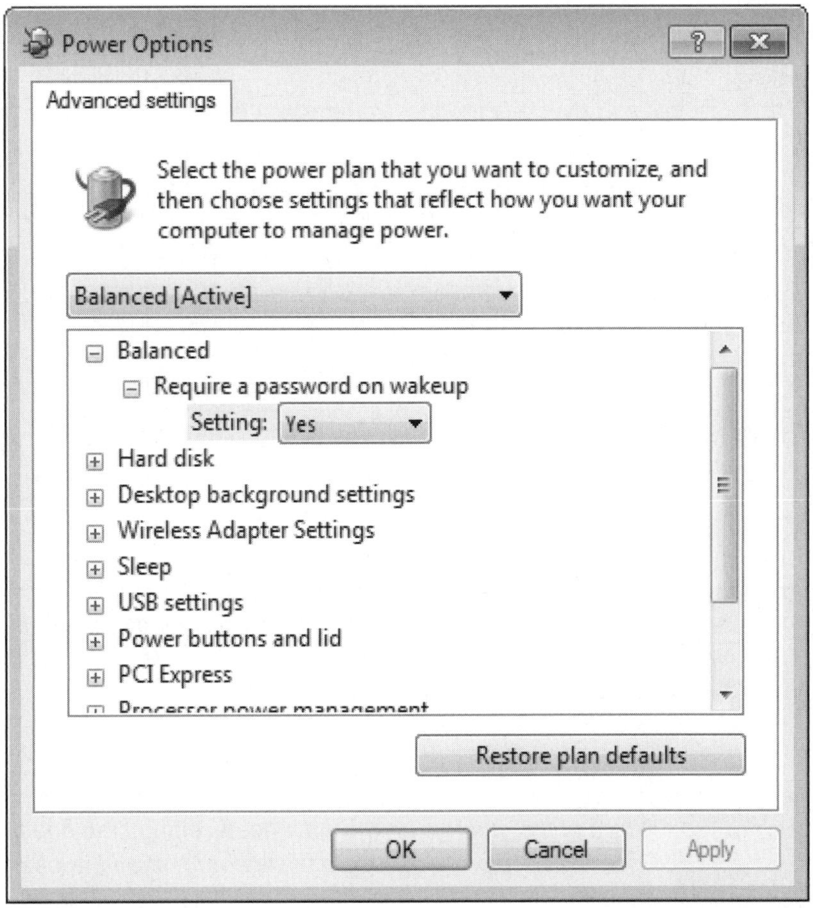

Figure 16-2
The Advanced Settings tab of the Power Options dialog box

9. Using the drop-down list to change power plans, examine the values for the advanced power settings and enter them in Table 16-4.

Table 16-4
Default Windows 7 advanced power configuration settings

Setting	Balanced	Power Saver	High Performance
Require a password on wakeup			
Turn off hard disk after			
Wireless Adapter Settings \ Power Saving Mode			
Sleep after			
Allow wake timers			
USB selective suspend setting			

(*continued*)

Table 16-4 (*continued*)

Power button action			
Link State Power Management			
Minimum processor state			
System cooling policy			
Maximum processor state			
Turn off display after			
When sharing media			
When playing video			

Question 4	*Which of the settings on the Advanced settings tab enables the High performance plan to achieve greater performance levels than the Balanced plan?*

Question 5	*Which of the settings on the Advanced settings tab enables the Power saver plan to conserve more energy than the other two plans?*

10. Click OK to close the Power Options dialog box.

11. Close the Power Options control panel.

12. Leave the workstation logged on for the next exercise.

Exercise 16.2   Creating a Custom Power Plan

Overview	In Exercise 16.2, you create power plans for your company's desktop and laptop workstations.
Completion time	20 minutes

1. Click Start. Then, click Control Panel. The Control Panel window appears.

2. Click Hardware and Sound > Power Options. The Power Options control panel appears.

3. Click Create a power plan. The Create a Power Plan Wizard appears, as shown in Figure 16-3.

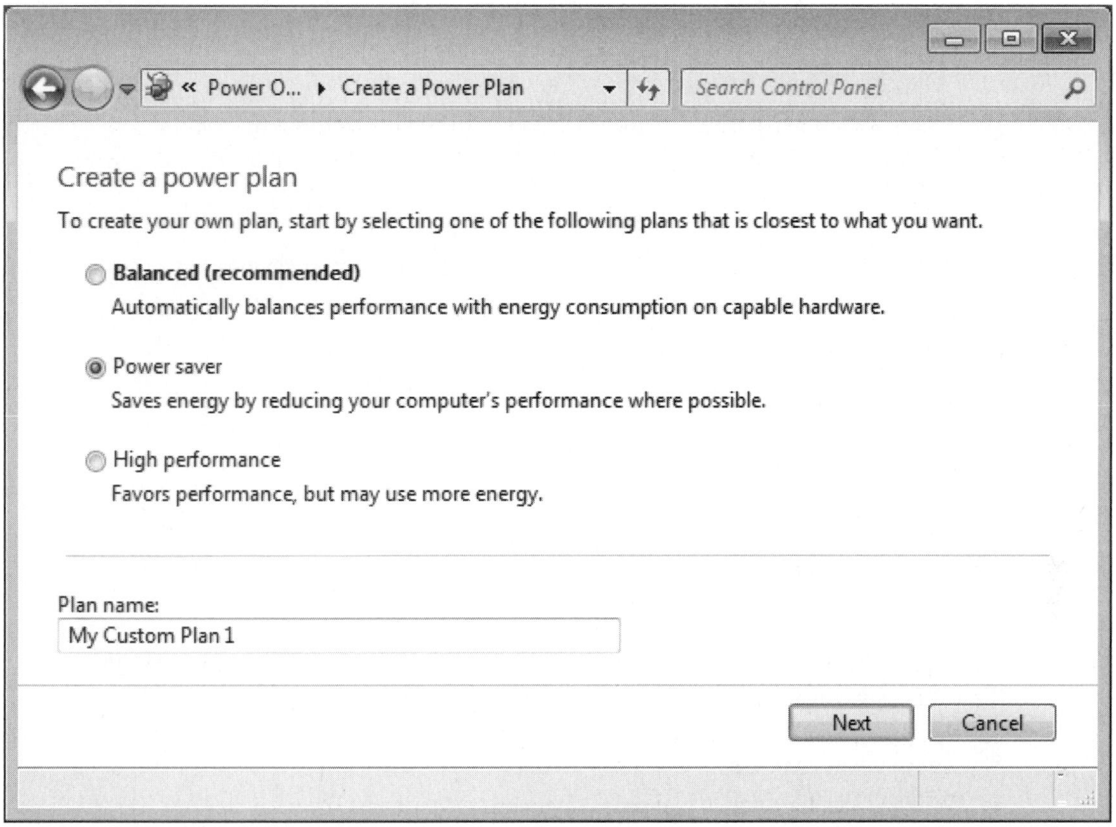

Figure 16-3
The Create a Power Plan Wizard

4. Leave the Balanced (recommended) option selected and, in the Plan name text box, type **NYC-CLa Desktops** and click Next. The *Change settings for the plan: NYC-CLa Desktops* page appears.

5. In the Turn off the display drop-down list, select **15 minutes**.

6. In the Put the computer to sleep drop-down list, select **30 minutes** and click Create. The NYC-CLa Desktops plan appears in the Power Options control panel.

7. Repeat steps 3 to 6 to create another power plan called **NYC-CLa Laptops** with the following settings:

    • Turn off the display: 5 minutes
    • Put the computer to sleep: 10 minutes

8. Take a screen shot of the Power Options control panel, showing the power plans you created, by pressing Alt+Prt Scr, and then paste the resulting image into the Lab16_worksheet file in the page provided by pressing Ctrl+V.

9.   Click the Change plan settings link for the NYC-CLa Desktops plan. The *Change settings for the plan: NYC-CLa Desktops* page appears.

10. Click Change advanced power settings. The Power Options dialog box appears, displaying the Advanced Settings tab.

11. Make sure that NYC-CLa Desktops is selected in the drop-down list and configure the following settings:

     - Turn off hard disk after: 15 minutes
     - PCI Express \ Link State Power Management: Maximum power savings
     - Processor power management \ Minimum processor state: 10%
     - Processor power management \ Maximum processor state: 85%
     - Multimedia settings \ When playing video: Optimize power settings

12. Click OK to close the Power Options dialog box.

13. Open the *Change settings for the plan: NYC-CLa Laptops* page, and then click Change advanced power settings. The Power Options dialog box appears, displaying the Advanced Settings tab.

14. Make sure that NYC-CLa Laptops is selected in the drop-down list and configure the following settings:

     - Turn off hard disk after: 5 minutes
     - Wireless adapter settings \ Power saving mode: Maximum power savings
     - PCI Express \ Link State Power Management: Maximum power savings
     - Processor power management \ Minimum processor state: 5%
     - Processor power management \ System cooling policy: Passive
     - Processor power management \ Maximum processor state: 65%
     - Multimedia settings \ When playing video: Optimize power settings

15. Click OK to close the Power Options dialog box.

Question 6	*Which of the settings you configured in both of your new power plans will prevent the computers from operating at peak performance levels?*

16. Close the Power Options control panel.

17. Leave the workstation logged on for the next exercise.

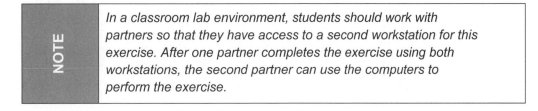

Exercise 16.3	Using Powercfg.exe
Overview	Now that you have created power plans for your company's desktop and laptop computers, you must determine how to transfer those plans to other computers. In Exercise 16.3, you use the Powercfg.exe command line utility to export your power plans from your NYC-CLa workstation and import them on NYC-CLb.
Completion time	10 minutes

> **NOTE**
>
> *In a classroom lab environment, students should work with partners so that they have access to a second workstation for this exercise. After one partner completes the exercise using both workstations, the second partner can use the computers to perform the exercise.*

1. Click Start. Then, click All Programs > Accessories. Right click Command Prompt and, from the context menu, select Run as administrator. An Administrator: Command Prompt window appears.

2. At the command prompt, type **powercfg–list** and press Enter. A list of the power plans on the computer appears, as shown in Figure 16-4.

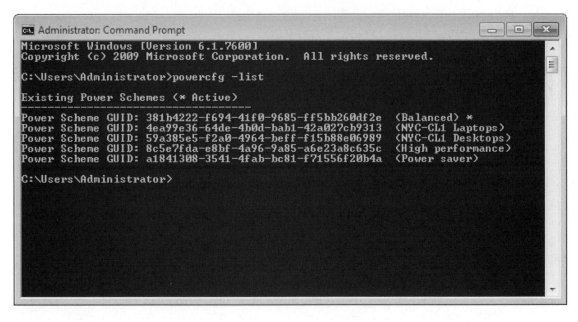

Figure 16-4
The Powercfg.exe plan list display

3. In Table 16-5, enter the 32-character GUID values for the power plans you created in Exercise 16.2, as displayed by Powercfg.exe.

Table 16-5
Custom power plan GUIDs

Power Plan Name	GUID
NYC-CLa Desktops	
NYC-CLa Laptops	

4. At the command prompt, type **powercfg –export nyc-cla-desktops.pow** *GUID*, where *GUID* is the 32-character value you entered in Table 16.5 for the NYC-CLa Desktops power plan. Then press Enter.

5. Next, type **powercfg –export nyc-cla-laptops.pow** *GUID*, where *GUID* is the 32-character value you entered in Table 16.5 for the NYC-CLa Laptops power plan. Then press Enter.

6. At the command prompt, type **copy *.pow \\rwdc01\downloads** and press Enter. The system copies your power plan files to the server.

7. On the NYC-CLb workstation, log on using the **contoso\Administrator** account and the password **Pa$$w0rd**.

8. Click Start. Then, click All Programs > Accessories. Right click Command Prompt and, from the context menu, select Run as administrator. An Administrator: Command Prompt window appears.

9. At the command prompt, type **powercfg –import \\rwdc01\downloads\nyc-cla-desktops.pow** and press Enter.

10. Then, type **powercfg –import \\rwdc01\downloads\nyc-cla-laptops.pow** and press Enter.

11. Take a screen shot of the Command Prompt window, showing the successful import commands, by pressing Alt+Prt Scr, and then paste the resulting image into the Lab16_worksheet file in the page provided by pressing Ctrl+V.

12. Click Start. Then, click Control Panel. The Control Panel window appears.

13. Click Hardware and Sound > Power Options. The Power Options control panel appears.

14. Click the Show additional plans down arrow. The additional plans appear, including the NYC-CLa Desktops and NYC-CLa Laptops plans you imported.

15. Log off of both workstations.

Exercise 16.4	Using BitLocker
Overview	In addition to investigating power settings, your director wants you to examine the BitLocker feature included in Windows 7. For Exercise 16.4, you will use BitLocker to encrypt an external drive connected to your workstation using a password.
Completion time	10 minutes

1. Connect the external drive to the computer by plugging it into an available USB port.

> **NOTE**
>
> *If you are working with an external hard drive that you have just connected to the workstation, you might have to initialize the disk in the Disk Management snap-in before you can proceed with the exercise.*

2. Click Start. Then, click Control Panel. The Control Panel window appears.

3. Click System and Security > BitLocker Drive Encryption. The BitLocker Drive Encryption control panel appears, as shown in Figure 16-5.

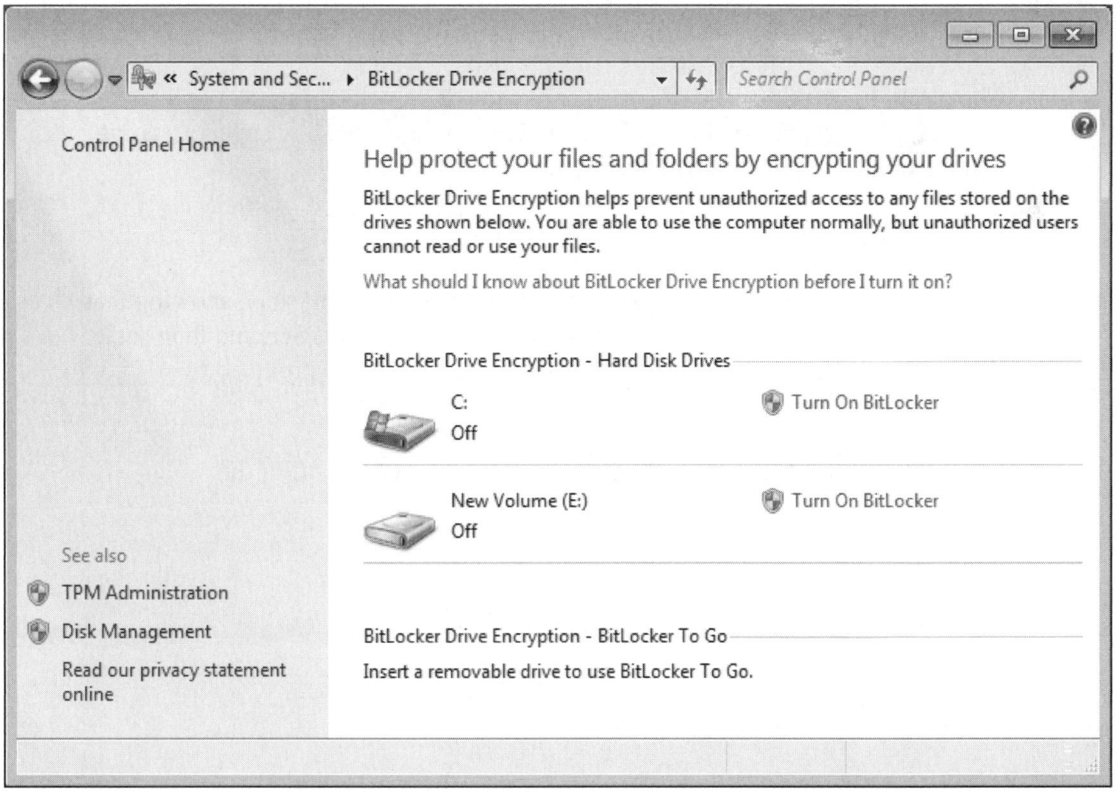

Figure 16-5
The BitLocker Drive Encryption control panel

4. Click the Turn On BitLocker link for your external drive. The BitLocker Drive Encryption Wizard appears, displaying the *Choose how you want to unlock this drive* page.

5. Select the Use a password to unlock this drive check box.

6. In the Type your password and Retype your password text boxes, type **Pa$$w0rd** and click Next. The *How do you want to store your recovery key?* page appears.

7. Click Save the recovery key to a file. The Save BitLocker Recovery Key as combo box appears.

8. Click Save to accept the default filename and location. A BitLocker Drive Encryption message box appears, confirming that you want to save the recovery key on the computer.

Question 7	*Under real-world conditions, why would it be unwise to store the recovery key on the computer?*

9. Click Yes. The wizard saves the recovery key.

10. Click Next. The *Are you ready to encrypt this drive?* page appears.

11. Click Start Encrypting. The wizard encrypts the drive, which can take several minutes, after which a BitLocker Drive Encryption message box appears, stating that the encryption of the drive is complete.

12. Click Close.

13. Take a screen shot of the BitLocker Drive Encryption control panel, showing that BitLocker is turned on for external drive, by pressing Alt+Prt Scr, and then paste the resulting image into the lab16_worksheet file in the page provided by pressing Ctrl+V.

14. Close the BitLocker Drive Encryption control panel and log off of the workstation.

LAB 17
CONFIGURING MOBILE CONNECTIVITY

This lab contains the following exercises and activities:

Exercise 17.1   Creating a VPN Connection

Exercise 17.2   Configuring a VPN Connection

Exercise 17.3   Connecting to a VPN Server

BEFORE YOU BEGIN

The lab environment consists of student workstations connected to a local area network, along with a server that functions as the domain controller for a domain called contoso.com. The computers required for this lab are listed in Table 17-1.

Table 17-1
Computers required for Lab 17

Computer	Operating System	Computer Name
Server	Windows Server 2008 R2	RWDC01
Workstation 1	Windows 7 Enterprise	NYC-CLa

NOTE

In a classroom lab environment, there will be one classroom server and the students will have workstations named using consecutive numbers in place of the a and b variables. In a virtual lab environment, each student will have three virtual machines, named RWDC01, NYC-CL1, and NYC-CL2.

In addition to the computers, you will also require the software listed in Table 17-2 to complete Lab 17.

Table 17-2
Software required for Lab 17

Software	Location
Lab 17 student worksheet	Lab17_worksheet.rtf (provided by instructor)

Working with Lab Worksheets

Each lab in this manual requires that you answer questions, shoot screen shots, and perform other activities that you will document in a worksheet named for the lab, such as Lab17_worksheet.rtf. Your instructor will provide you with access to the worksheets. It is recommended that you use a USB flash drive to store your worksheets, so that you can submit them to your instructor for review. As you perform the exercises in each lab, open the appropriate worksheet file using WordPad, fill in the required information, and save the file to your flash drive.

SCENARIO

Contoso, Ltd. is implementing a virtual private networking server that will enable users traveling or working from home to connect to the company network through the Internet. As part of the testing phase of the project, your assignment is to create a VPN client connection on a Windows 7 workstation and examine the configuration settings the operating system provides.

After completing this lab, you will be able to:

- Create a VPN connection

- Configure VPN connection settings

- Establish a connection to a VPN server

Estimated lab time: 40 minutes

Exercise 17.1	Creating a VPN Connection
Overview	In Exercise 17.1, you create a connection that enables the workstation to connect to your RWDC01 server using virtual private networking.
Completion time	15 minutes

1. Turn on the NYC-CLa workstation and log on using the **contoso\Administrator** account and the password **Pa$$w0rd**.

2. Click Start. Then, click Control Panel. The Control Panel window appears.

3. Click Network and Internet > Network and Sharing Center. The Network and Sharing Center control panel appears, as shown in Figure 17-1.

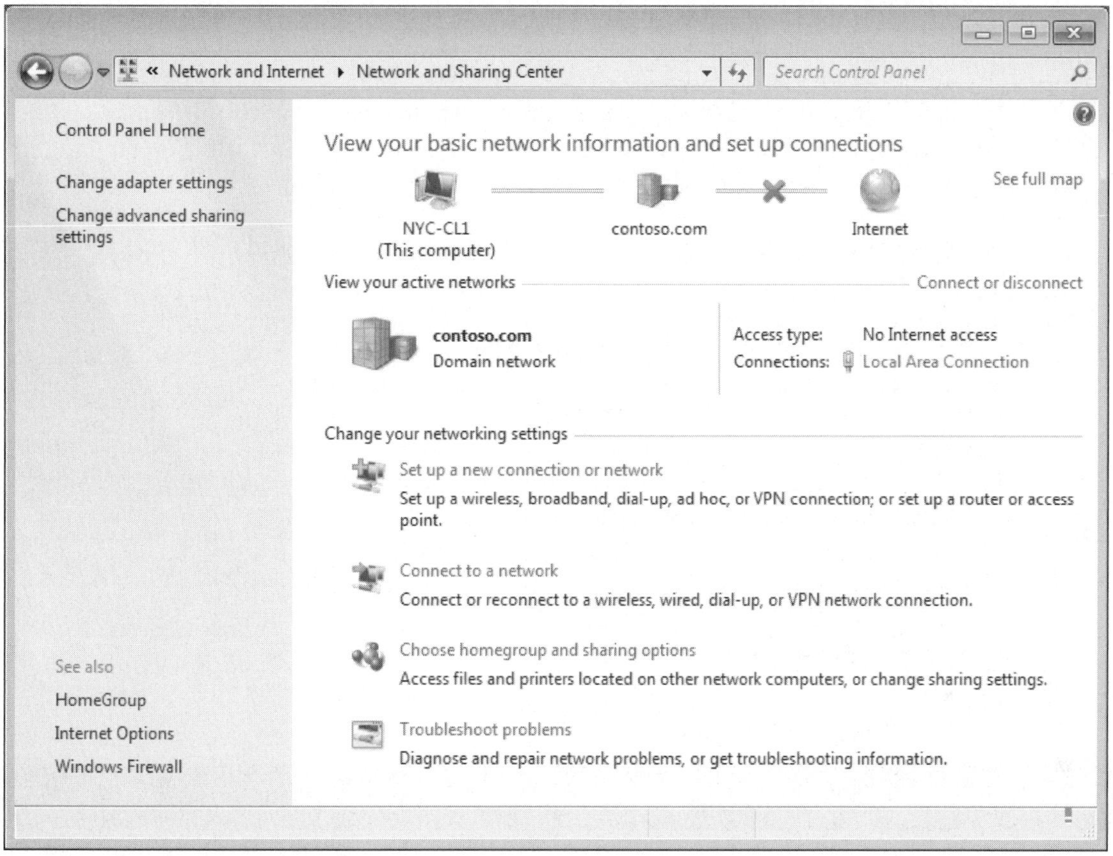

Figure 17-1
The Network and Sharing Center control panel

4. Click Set up a new connection or network. The Set Up a Connection or Network Wizard appears, displaying the *Choose a connection option* page.

5. Select Connect to a workplace and click Next. The *How do you want to connect?* page appears.

6. Click Use my Internet connection (VPN). The *Do you want to set up an Internet connection before continuing?* page appears.

	In a classroom lab environment, *the* Do you want to set up an Internet connection before continuing? *page does not appear if the network is already connected to the Internet. In a virtual lab environment, the virtual network is not connected to the Internet, but you will bypass the Internet link for the purposes of this lab.*

7. Click I'll set up an Internet connection later. The *Type the Internet address to connect to* page appears.

8. In the Internet address text box, type **rwdc01.contoso.com**.

9. In the Destination name text box, type **VPN Server Connection**.

10. Select the Allow other people to use this connection check box and click Next. The *Type your user name and password* page appears.

11. In the User name text box, type **Administrator**.

12. In the Password text box, type **Pa$$w0rd**.

13. In the Domain (optional) text box, type **contoso** and click Create. A *The connection is ready to use* page appears.

14. Click Close.

15. Leave the workstation logged on for the next exercise.

Exercise 17.2	Configuring a VPN Connection
Overview	In Exercise 17.2, you examine the parameters you can use to configure the VPN connection you created in Exercise 17.1. Because the VPN server will at first have only a limited number of connections, you must prevent users from remaining connected when they are not actually using the network.
Completion time	5 minutes

1. On the Network and Sharing Center control panel, click Change adapter settings. The Network Connections window appears.

Question 1	*How many connections are there in the Network Connections window?*

2. Right click the VPN Server Connection icon and, from the context menu, select Properties. The VPN Server Connection Properties sheet appears.

3. Take a screen shot of the VPN Server Connection Properties sheet by pressing Alt+Prt Scr, and then paste the resulting image into the Lab17_worksheet file in the page provided by pressing Ctrl+V.

4. Click the Options tab.

5. From the Idle time before hanging up drop-down list, select **5 minutes**.

6. Clear the Redial if line is dropped check box and click OK to close the VPN Server Connection Properties sheet.

7. Leave the workstation logged on for the next exercise.

Exercise 17.3	Connecting to a VPN Server
Overview	In Exercise 17.3, you practice establishing a connection to the VPN server.
Completion time	20 minutes

1. Open the Network and Sharing Center control panel and click Connect to a network. A pop-up window appears above the notification area.

2. Click the VPN Server Connection link. A Connect button appears.

3. Click Connect. A Connect VPN Server Connection dialog box appears, as shown in Figure 17-2.

Figure 17-2
The Connection VPN Server Connection dialog box

4. In the Password text box, type **Pa$$w0rd** and click Connect.

5. The workstation connects to the VPN server and the connection appears on the Network and Sharing Center control panel.

6. Take a screen shot of the Network and Sharing Center control panel, showing the VPN connection, by pressing Alt+Prt Scr, and then paste the resulting image into the Lab17_worksheet file in the page provided by pressing Ctrl+V.

7. Click the VPN Server Connection link. The VPN Server Connection Status dialog box appears.

8. Click the Details tab (not the Details button).

Question 2	Which of the VPN protocols is the connection using?

Question 3	Which authentication protocol is the VPN connection using?

9. Click the General tab, and then click Properties. The VPN Server Connection Properties sheet appears.

10. Click the Security tab.

11. In the Type of VPN drop-down list, select Point-to-Point Tunneling Protocol (PPTP) and click OK. A Network Connections message box appears, informing you that the connection is currently active.

12. Click OK.

13. On the VPN Server Connection Status dialog box, click Disconnect. The dialog box closes.

14. Try again to connect to the VPN server, as you did in Steps 2 through 4.

15. Enter the result of the connection attempt in the appropriate cell in Table 17-3.

Table 17-3
Connection results for VPN protocols

Type of VPN	Result message
Point-to-Point Tunneling Protocol	
Layer 2 Tunneling Protocol with IPsec (L2TP/IPSec)	
Secure Socket Tunneling Protocol (SSTP)	
IKEv2	

16. Configure the VPN Server Connection to use each of the three remaining VPN protocols in turn, and enter the resulting connection messages in Table 17-3.

17. Reconfigure the VPN Server Connection to use PPTP and establish a connection to the server.

18. Open the Network Connections window.

19. Right click the Local Area Connection icon and, from the context menu, select Properties. The Local Area Connection Properties sheet appears.

20. Select Internet Protocol Version 4 (TCP/IPv4) and click Properties. The Internet Protocol Version 4 (TCP/IPv4) Properties sheet appears.

21. Change the IP Address value from 10.10.0.x to **10.10.3.x**. Then double click OK to close the two Properties sheets.

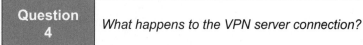

Question 4	What happens to the VPN server connection?

22. Reconfigure the VPN Server Connection to use IKEv2 and establish a connection to the server.

23. Open the Internet Protocol Version 4 (TCP/IPv4) Properties sheet again and change the IP Address from 10.10.3.x back to **10.10.0.x.**

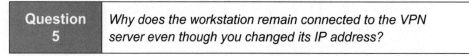

Question 5	Why does the workstation remain connected to the VPN server even though you changed its IP address?

24. Right click the VPN Server Connection and, from the context menu, select Disconnect. The workstation disconnects from the server.

25. Log off of the workstation.

LAB 18
TROUBLESHOOTING WINDOWS 7

This lab contains the following exercises and activities:

Exercise 18.1   Troubleshooting Network Connectivity

Exercise 18.2   Troubleshooting Disk Access

Exercise 18.3   Troubleshooting Shared Folders

Exercise 18.4   Troubleshooting Logon Problems

BEFORE YOU BEGIN

The lab environment consists of student workstations connected to a local area network, along with a server that functions as the domain controller for a domain called contoso.com. The computers required for this lab are listed in Table 18-1.

Table 18-1
Computers required for Lab 18

Computer	Operating System	Computer Name
Server	Windows Server 2008 R2	RWDC01
Workstation 1	Windows 7 Enterprise	NYC-CLa
Workstation 2	Windows 7 Enterprise	NYC-CLb
Workstation 3	Windows 7 Enterprise	NYC-CLc
Workstation 4	Windows 7 Enterprise	NYC-CLd

This lab consists of four computing scenarios in which you play the role of a help desk technician who is required to troubleshoot problems reported by Windows 7 users. Each of the Windows 7 workstations has been configured to malfunction in some way, and it is your job, based on the information in each scenario, to diagnose the problem and solve it.

In a classroom lab environment, each of the workstations in the classroom has been marked with a number from 1 to 4. To complete each scenario, you must go to a workstation bearing the same number as the exercise, start Windows 7, log on using the **contoso\Administrator** account and the password **Pa$$w0rd**, and troubleshoot the problem described in the scenario using only the tools provided with the operating system. The problems will be software related; in none of the scenarios will it be necessary to open the computer case.

In a virtual lab environment, there are four workstations with the names NYC-CL1, NYC-CL2, NYC-CL3, and NYC-CL4. Each of the exercises in the workstations corresponds to the lab exercise with the same number. To complete each scenario, you access the workstation bearing the same number as the exercise, start Windows 7, log on using the **contoso\Administrator** account and the password **Pa$$w0rd**, and troubleshoot the problem described in the scenario using only the tools provided with the operating system.

In this lab, the process is just as important as the results. As you work with each computer, you must keep a detailed troubleshooting log in your Lab 18 worksheet that includes everything you checked, everything you found, and everything you did. Keep detailed notes regarding the tools you used, how you used them, and the results of your tests. Once you have arrived at a solution to the problem described in the scenario, document the exact procedure for repairing the system in your log. Do not share your work with other students.

In a classroom lab, once you have completed the troubleshooting process, you must return the computer to the same state in which you found it and shut the computer down. In other words, after fixing each computer, you must break it again so that another student can troubleshoot the same problem on it. When you have completed all four troubleshooting scenarios, submit your logs to your instructor.

> **NOTE**
>
> *In a classroom lab environment, there will be one classroom server and the students will have workstations named using consecutive numbers in place of the a, b, c, and d variables. In a virtual lab environment, each student will have five virtual machines, named RWDC01, NYC-CL1, NYC-CL2, NYC-CL3, and NYC-CL4.*

In addition to the computers, you will also require the software listed in Table 18-2 to complete Lab 18.

Table 18-2
Software required for Lab 18

Software	Location
Lab 18 student worksheet	Lab18_worksheet.rtf (provided by instructor)

Working with Lab Worksheets

Each lab in this manual requires that you answer questions, shoot screen shots, and perform other activities that you will document in a worksheet named for the lab, such as Lab18_worksheet.rtf. Your instructor will provide you with access to the worksheets. It is recommended that you use a USB flash drive to store your worksheets, so that you can submit them to your instructor for review. As you perform the exercises in each lab, open the appropriate worksheet file using WordPad, fill in the required information, and save the file to your flash drive.

SCENARIO

You are a desktop technician for Contoso, Ltd., working at the Windows 7 help desk. When a user calls or emails you with a computer problem, it is your job to travel to that user's workstation and resolve it. To account for your time and to build up a company troubleshooting database, you must document each of your calls as well as the troubleshooting process for each computer on which you work.

After completing this lab, you will be able to:

■ Troubleshoot a variety of Windows 7 configuration problems

Estimated lab time: 80 minutes

Exercise 18.1	Troubleshooting Network Connectivity
Overview	Rob calls the help desk to report that he cannot access any Web sites on the Internet. While he is still on the phone, you have him try to access a file on his departmental server. In both cases, his attempts fail. Troubleshoot Rob's computer and determine why he is unable to access the network. The troubleshooting process will be completed when you are able to access the network using Rob's computer.
Completion time	20 minutes

Exercise 18.2	Troubleshooting Disk Access
Overview	Alice sends an email to the help desk stating that when she tried to copy some files to her X: drive, which is a volume on her local hard disk, she was unable to do so. Because Alice has already left for her vacation, she cannot provide any more details about the problem, but she writes that she would appreciate the problem being fixed by the time she returns. The troubleshooting process will be completed when Alice can write files to her X: drive.
Completion time	20 minutes

Exercise 18.3	Troubleshooting Shared Folders
Overview	Gail is the head bookkeeper for your company, and she stores the firm's financial spreadsheet files on her Windows 7 computer. The other bookkeepers in the department, who all have user accounts that are members of the local Users group, work with the spreadsheets on Gail's computer by accessing two shared folders called Payable and Receivable. Gail has just called the help desk and reported that since having a new network adapter installed, the other bookkeepers have been unable to access the shares. However, Gail is able to access Web sites on the Internet. The troubleshooting process will be completed when other computers on the network are able to read files from and write them to the Payable and Receivable shares on Gail's computer using the local Student user account and the password Pa$$w0rd.
Completion time	20 minutes

Exercise 18.4	Troubleshooting Logon Problems
Overview	Sarah calls the help desk because she has an intermittent problem logging on to her computer using the local Student user account and the password Pa$$w0rd. Some mornings, she logs on without a problem. On other days, she cannot log on at first, but after waiting a few minutes, her logon is successful. This morning, it took three attempts over the course of 30 minutes before she was able to log on, and she is becoming extremely frustrated. The troubleshooting process will be completed when Sarah is able to log on to her computer consistently with no delays.
Completion time	20 minutes

APPENDIX: LAB SETUP GUIDE

The Microsoft *Windows 7 Configuration* title of the Microsoft Official Academic Course (MOAC) series includes two books: a textbook and a lab manual. The exercises in the lab manual are designed either for a virtual machine environment or for classroom use under the supervision of an instructor or lab aide. In an academic setting, the computer lab might be used by a variety of classes each day, so you must plan your setup procedure accordingly. For example, consider automating the classroom setup procedure and using removable hard disks in the classroom. You can use the automated setup procedure to rapidly configure the classroom environment, and remove the fixed disks after teaching this class each day.

NOTE	*This appendix describes the process by which instructors teaching the course in a standard wired classroom lab should set up and install the servers and workstations the students will need to complete the exercises in the lab manual. This setup guide can also be adapted for use with a workstation-based virtual machine environment, such as Microsoft Virtual PC, with each student computer running the required server and workstations. For instructors using MOAC Labs Online, no setup or installation is necessary, as the virtual machines in the online labs are pre-configured and ready for the students to use.*

LAB CONFIGURATION

This course should be taught in a lab containing networked computers where students can develop their skills through hands-on experience with Microsoft Windows 7. The exercises in the lab manual require the computers to be installed and configured in a specific manner. Failure to adhere to the setup instructions in this document can produce unanticipated results when the students perform the exercises.

The lab configuration consists of a single server running Microsoft Windows Server 2008 R2 Enterprise and a number of workstations that run Windows Vista at the outset, and which later will run Windows 7 Enterprise.

The lab computers are located on an isolated network, configured as an Active Directory Domain Services (AD DS) domain separate from the rest of the school or organization network. The lab server functions as an Active Directory Domain Services domain controller, as well as performing a number of other roles at various times throughout the course.

The lab uses the following information for the AD DS and server configuration:

- Active Directory Domain Services domain name: contoso.com
- Computer name: RWDC01
- Fully qualified domain name (FQDN): rwdc01.contoso.com

This document includes a setup procedure that configures the server to provide all of the infrastructure services required throughout the course. Once you have completed the initial setup, no further modifications to the lab server should be necessary.

The workstations in the lab are named NYC-CL*xx*, where *xx* is a unique number assigned to each computer. Each workstation will be a member of the contoso.com domain throughout most of the exercises, and also have a local administrative account called Student.

> NOTE
>
> *For the purposes of this lab, all server and workstation passwords, for user acounts and other purposes, will be set to* **Pa$$w0rd***. This is obviously not a secure practice in a real-world situation, and instructors should remind students of this at the outset.*

The initial workstation setup consists only of a standard Windows Vista installation, and the joining of the computer to the contoso.com domain. During the course of the labs, the students will be responsible for installing Windows 7 on the workstations, modifying the domain membership as needed for each exercise, and performing any other configuration tasks required to complete the exercises.

Some of the lab exercises have dependencies on previous exercises, as noted in the lab manual and the instructor notes for each exercise. Students should perform the lab exercises in order, and might have to complete any exercises they have missed due to absence before proceeding to the next lab.

Server Requirements

The computer running Windows Server 2008 R2 in the classroom requires the following hardware and software:

Hardware Requirements

- Minimum: 1.4 GHz x64 processor
- Minimum: 512 MB RAM (2 GB recommended)
- Minimum: 32 GB
- DVD drive
- Network interface adapter
- Minimum: Super VGA (800x600) display
- Keyboard
- Mouse

Software Requirements

All of the software listed is required on the server:

- Microsoft Windows Server 2008 R2 Enterprise: Evaluation edition available as a free download from Microsoft's web site at http://www.microsoft.com/windowsserver2008/en/us/trial-software.aspx

- Windows 7 Upgrade Advisor: Download Windows7UpgradeAdvisorSetup.exe from http://www.microsoft.com/downloads/details.aspx?displaylang=en&FamilyID=1b544e90-7659-4bd9-9e51-2497c146af15

- Windows Easy Transfer for transferring from Windows Vista (32-bit) to Windows 7: Download Windows6.0-KB928635-x86.msu from http://www.microsoft.com/downloads/details.aspx?familyid=09D80814-2A73-4245-A63B-8E780D0430CB&displaylang=en

- Windows Easy Transfer for transferring from Windows Vista (64-bit) to Windows 7: Download Windows6.0-KB928635-x64.msu from http://www.microsoft.com/downloads/details.aspx?familyid=30C4DA6D-0522-4D28-AAC3-CE9D70AC6A6A&displaylang=en

- Windows 7 Automated Installation Kit: Download KB3AIK_EN.iso from http://www.microsoft.com/downloads/details.aspx?displaylang=en&FamilyID=696dd665-9f76-4177-a811-39c26d3b3b34

- Microsoft Deployment Toolkit 2010: Download MicrosoftDeploymentToolkit2010_x86.msi and/or MicrosoftDeploymentToolkit2010_x64.msi from http://www.microsoft.com/downloads/details.aspx?familyid=3BD8561F-77AC-4400-A0C1-FE871C461A89&displaylang=en

- Remote Server Administration Tools for Windows 7: Download x86fre_GRMRSAT_MSU.msu and/or amd64fre_GRMRSATX_MSU.msu from http://www.microsoft.com/downloads/details.aspx?displaylang=en&FamilyID=7d2f6ad7-656b-4313-a005-4e344e43997d

- Windows 7 Enterprise Edition

With the exception of the Windows Server 2008 R2 operating system itself, the software products listed here do not have to be installed on the server. You must, however, download them and make them available to the workstation on a server share. The students will install each of these products at various points in the course.

Workstation Requirements

Each workstation requires the following hardware and software:

Hardware Requirements

- Minimum: 1 GHz 32-bit (x86) or 64-bit (x64) processor
- Minimum: 1 GB RAM (32-bit) / 2 GB RAM (64-bit)
- Minimum: 40 GB hard drive
- DVD drive
- Network interface adapter
- Minimum: Super VGA (800x600) display
- Keyboard
- Mouse

Software Requirements

All of the software listed is required for the course:

- Windows Vista Business or Enterprise Edition
- Windows 7 Enterprise Edition

> *Each of the student workstations can run either the 32-bit or 64-bit version of Windows, as long as the computer has the appropriate hardware for the operating system and you provide each workstation with the additional software it needs in the version of the appropriate platform.*

SERVER SETUP INSTRUCTIONS

Before you begin, do the following:

- Read this entire document.
- Make sure you have the installation disks for Microsoft Windows Server 2008 R2, Microsoft Windows Vista, and Microsoft Windows 7.

Installing the Lab Server

Overview	Using the following procedure, install Windows Server 2008 R2 on RWDC01. This procedure assumes that you are performing a clean installation of the Windows Server 2008 R2 Enterprise evaluation edition, and that, if you have downloaded an image file, you have already burned it to a DVD-ROM disk.
Completion time	20 minutes

> *By performing the following setup instructions, your computer's hard disks will be repartitioned and reformatted. You will lose all existing data on these systems.*

1. Turn the computer on and insert the Windows Server 2008 R2 installation DVD into the drive.

2. Press any key, if necessary, to boot from the DVD-ROM disk. The Setup program loads, and the Install Windows window appears.

3. Modify the *Language to install, Time and currency format*, and *Keyboard or input method* settings, if necessary, and click Next.

4. Click Install Now. The *Select the operating system you want to install* page appears.

5. Select Windows Server 2008 R2 Enterprise (Full Installation) and click Next. The *Please read the license terms page* appears.

6. Select the *I accept the license terms* check box and click Next. The *Which type of installation do you want?* page appears.

7. Click Custom (advanced). The *Where do you want to install Windows?* page appears.

8. Select Disk 0 Unallocated Space and click Next. The *Installing Windows* page appears, indicating the progress of the Setup program as it installs the operating system. After the installation completes and the computer restarts, a message appears stating that *The user's password must be changed before logging on the first time*.

9. Click OK. A Windows logon screen appears.

10. In the *New password* and *Confirm password* text boxes, type **Pa$$w0rd** and click the right-arrow button. A message appears, stating that *Your password has been changed*.

11. Click OK. The logon process completes and the Initial Configuration Tasks window appears.

Once the installation process is finished, you must complete the following tasks to configure the server and install the necessary roles to support the student workstations.

Completing Initial Server Configuration Tasks	
Overview	Complete the following configuration tasks before you install Active Directory Domain Services or any other roles on the server.
Completion time	10 minutes

Configuring Date and Time Settings

1. In the Initial Configuration Tasks window, click Set time zone. The Date and Time dialog box appears.

2. If the time and/or date shown in the dialog box are not correct, click Change date and time and, in the Date and Time Settings dialog box, set the correct date and time and click OK.

3. If the time zone is not correct for your location, click Change time zone and, in the Time Zone Settings dialog box, set the correct time zone and click OK.

Configuring TCP/IP Settings

1. In the Initial Configuration Tasks window, click Configure networking. The Network Connections window appears.

2. Right click the Local Area Connection icon and, from the context menu, select Properties. The Local Area Connection Properties sheet appears.

3. Select Internet Protocol Version 4 (TCP/IPv4) and click Properties. The Internet Protocol Version 4 (TCP/IPv4) Properties sheet appears.

4. Select the *Use the following IP address* option and configure the following settings:

   - IP address: 10.10.0.2
   - Subnet mask: 255.0.0.0
   - Default gateway: Leave blank
   - Preferred DNS server: 10.10.0.2
   - Alternate DNS server: Leave blank

5. Click OK to close the Internet Protocol Version 4 (TCP/IPv4) Properties sheet.

6. Click Close to close the Local Area Connection Properties sheet.

7. Close the Network Connections window.

Naming the Server

1. In the Initial Configuration Tasks window, click Provide computer name and domain. The System Properties sheet appears.

2. Click Change. The Computer Name/Domain Changes dialog box appears.

3. In the *Computer name* text box, type **RWDC01** and click OK.

4. A Computer Name/Domain Changes message box appears, stating that you must restart the computer.

5. Click OK.

6. Click Close to close the System Properties dialog box. A Microsoft Windows message box appears, instructing you to restart the computer again.

7. Click Restart Now. The system restarts.

Installing Server Roles

Overview	After configuring the Windows server, you can begin to install the server roles needed to support the student workstation, as described in the following sections.
Completion time	45 minutes

Installing Active Directory Domain Services

1. Log on to the server using the **Administrator** account and the password **Pa$$w0rd**. The Initial Configuration Tasks window appears.

2. Under Customize This Server, click Add roles. The Add Roles Wizard appears.

3. Click Next to bypass the *Before You Begin* page. The *Select Server Roles* page appears.

4. Select the Active Directory Domain Services check box. The *Add features required for Active Directory Domain Services?* dialog box appears.

5. Click Add Required Features. Then click Next. The *Introduction to Active Directory Domain Services* page appears.

6. Click Next. The *Confirm Installation Selections* page appears.

7. Click Install. The *Installation Results* page appears.

8. Click Close this wizard and launch the Active Directory Domain Services Installation Wizard (dcpromo.exe). The Active Directory Domain Services Installation Wizard appears.

9. Click Next to bypass the *Welcome* page. The *Operating System Compatibility* page appears.

10. Click Next. The *Choose a Deployment Configuration* page appears.

11. Select the Create a new domain in a new forest option and click Next. The *Name the Forest Root Domain* page appears.

12. In the FWDN of the forest root domain text box, type **contoso.com** and click Next. The *Set Forest Functional Level* page appears.

13. In the Forest functional level drop-down list, select Windows Server 2008 R2 and click Next. The *Additional Domain Controller options* page appears.

14. Click Next. An Active Directory Domain Services Installation Wizard message box appears.

15. Click Yes. The *Location for Database, Log Files, and SYSVOL* page appears.

16. Click Next. The *Directory Services Restore Mode Administrator Password* page appears.

17. In the Password and Confirm password text boxes, type **Pa$$w0rd** and click Next. The *Summary* page appears.

18. Click Next. The wizard installs Active Directory Domain Services. The *Completing the Active Directory Domain Services Installation Wizard* page appears.

19. Click Finish. Then click Restart Now. The computer restarts.

Installing Active Directory Certificate Services

1. Log on to the server using the Administrator account and the password Pa$$w0rd. The Initial Configuration Tasks window appears.

2. Under Customize This Server, click *Add roles*. The Add Roles Wizard appears.

3. Click Next to bypass the *Before You Begin* page. The *Select Server Roles* page appears.

4. Select the Active Directory Certificate Services check box and click Next. The *Introduction to Active Directory Certificate Services* page appears.

5. Click Next. The *Select Role Services* page appears.

6. Select the Certification Authority Web Enrollment check box. The *Add role services and features required for Certification Authority Web Enrollment?* dialog box appears.

7. Click Add Required Role Services. Then click Next. The *Specify Setup Type* page appears.

8. Click Next to accept the default Enterprise option. The *Specify CA Type* page appears.

9. Click Next to accept the default Root CA option. The *Set Up Private Key* page appears.

10. Click Next to accept the default settings. The *Configure Cryptography for CA* page appears.

11. Click Next to accept the default settings. The *Configure CA Name* page appears.

12. Click Next to accept the default settings. The *Set Validity Period* page appears.

13. Click Next to accept the default settings. The *Configure Certificate Database* page appears.

14. Click Next to accept the default settings. The *Web Server (IIS)* page appears.

15. Click Next. The *Select Role Services* page appears.

16. Click Next to accept the default settings. The *Confirm Installation Selections* page appears.

17. Click Install. The wizard installs the selected role services and the *Installation Results* page appears.

18. Click Close.

Installing DHCP Server

1. In the Initial Configuration Tasks window, under Customize This Server, click Add roles. The Add Roles Wizard appears.

2. Click Next to bypass the *Before You Begin* page. The *Select Server Roles* page appears.

3. Select the DHCP Server check box and click Next. The *Introduction to DHCP Server* page appears.

4. Click Next. The *Select Network Connection Bindings* page appears.

5. Click Next to accept the default settings. The *Specify IPv4 DNS Server Settings* page appears.

6. Click Next to accept the default settings. The *Specify IPv4 WINS Server Settings* page appears.

7. Click Next to accept the default settings. The *Add or Edit DHCP Scopes* page appears.

8. Click Add. The Add Scope dialog box appears.

9. Complete the fields in the dialog box using the following values and click OK:

    *   Scope name: contoso.com
    *   Starting IP address: 10.10.0.100
    *   Ending IP address: 10.10.0.199
    *   Subnet mask: 255.0.0.0
    *   Default gateway (optional): Leave blank

10. Click Next. The *Configure DHCPv6 Stateless Mode* page appears.

11. Click Next to accept the default settings. The *Specify IPv6 DNS Server Settings* page appears.

12. Click Next to accept the default settings. The *Authorize DHCP Server* page appears.

13. Click Next to accept the default settings. The *Confirm Installation Selections* page appears.

14. Click Install. The wizard installs the role and the *Installation Results* page appears.

15. Click Close.

Installing Routing and Remote Access

1. In the Initial Configuration Tasks window, under Customize This Server, click Add roles. The Add Roles Wizard appears.

2.   Click Next to bypass the *Before You Begin* page. The *Select Server Roles* page appears.

3.   Select the Network Policy and Access Services check box and click Next. The *Introduction to Network Policy and Access Services* page appears.

4.   Click Next. The *Select Role Services* page appears.

5.   Select the Routing and Remote Access Services check box and click Next. The *Confirm Installation selections* page appears.

6.   Click Install. The *Installation Results* page appears.

7.   Click Close.

8.   Click Start. Then click Administrative Tools > Routing and Remote Access. The Routing and Remote Access console appears.

9.   Right click the RWDC01 (local) node and, from the context menu, select Configure and Enable Routing and Remote Access. The Routing and Remote Access Server Setup Wizard appears.

10.   Click Next to bypass the *Welcome* page. The *Configuration* page appears.

11.   Select the Custom configuration option and click Next. The *Custom Configuration* page appears.

12.   Select the VPN access check box and click Next. The *Completing the Routing and Remote Access Server Setup Wizard* page appears.

13.   Click Finish. A Routing and Remote Access message box appears.

14.   Click Start service. The wizard configures Routing and Remote Access and starts the service.

15.   Close the Routing and Remote Access console.

Install Windows Deployment Services

1.   In the Initial Configuration Tasks window, under Customize This Server, click Add roles. The Add Roles Wizard appears.

2.   Click Next to bypass the *Before You Begin* page. The *Select Server Roles* page appears.

3.   Select the Windows Deployment Services check box and click Next. The *Introduction to Windows Deployment Services* page appears.

4.   Click Next. The *Select Role Services* page appears.

5.   Click Next to accept the default settings. The *Confirm Installation Selections* page appears.

6. Click Install. The wizard installs the role and the *Installation Results* page appears.

7. Click Close.

8. Click Start. Then click Administrative Tools > Windows Deployment Services. The Windows Deployment Services console appears.

9. Expand the Servers node.

10. Right click the RWDC01.contoso.com node and, from the context menu, select Configure Server. The Windows Deployment Services Configuration Wizard appears.

11. Click Next to bypass the *Before You Begin* page. The *Remote Installation Folder Location* page appears.

12. Click Next to accept the default setting. A warning box appears.

13. Click Yes to continue. The *DHCP Option 60* page appears.

14. Select the Do not listen on port 67 and Configure DHCP option 60 to 'PXEClient' check boxes and click Next. The *PXE Server Initial Settings* page appears.

15. Select the Respond to all client computers (known and unknown) option and click Next. The *Operation Complete* page appears.

16. Leave the Add images to the server now check box selected and click Finish. The Add Image Wizard appears, displaying the *Image File* page.

17. Insert a Windows 7 Enterprise installation disk into the DVD drive.

18. In the Path text box, type **D:** where D is the drive letter assigned to the computer's DVD drive. Then click Next. The *Image Group* page appears.

19. Click Next to accept the default setting. The *Review Settings* page appears.

20. Click Next. The *Task Progress* page appears as the wizard adds the images from the disk to the WDS server.

21. Click Finish.

22. Close the Windows Deployment Services console.

Preparing the Server File System

Overview	The student workstations in the lab do not require access to the Internet, as long as the software the students need to install as they complete the exercises is available on the lab server. To prepare the server, complete the following procedure.
Completion time	15 minutes

1. Download all of the free software products listed in the Software Requirements section (pp. 192–193).

2. On the RWDC01 server, open Windows Explorer and create a new folder on the C: drive called **downloads**.

3. Share the downloads folder using the name *downloads.*

4. Assign the Allow Full Control share permission to the Everyone special identity.

5. Copy the Windows 7 Upgrade Advisor, Windows Easy Transfer, Microsoft Deployment Toolkit, and Remote Server Administration Tools for Windows 7 installation files you downloaded to the c:\downloads folder you created.

6. Burn the Windows 7 Automated Installation Kit image file you downloaded to a DVD-ROM disk.

7. Insert the Windows 7 AIK disk into the computer's DVD drive.

8. Create a subfolder called **win7aik** under the c:\downloads folder you created earlier.

9. Copy the entire contents of the Windows 7 AIK disk to the c:\downloads\win7aik folder.

10. Insert your Windows 7 Enterprise installation disk into the computer's DVD drive.

11. Create a subfolder called **win7ent** under the c:\downloads folder you created earlier.

12. Copy the entire contents of the Windows 7 Enterprise disk to the c:\downloads\win7ent folder.

WORKSTATION SETUP INSTRUCTIONS

Installing a Lab Workstation	
Overview	All of the workstations in the lab will initially be installed with Windows Vista Enterprise. As the students progress through the lab exercises, they will practice upgrading Vista workstations to Windows 7 and performing clean Windows 7 installations. To prepare the workstations for the students' first use, you must install and configure each one as follows.
Completion time	20 minutes

1. Turn the computer on and insert the Windows Vista Enterprise installation DVD into the drive.

2. Press any key, if necessary, to boot from the DVD-ROM disk. The Setup program loads, and the Install Windows window appears.

3. Modify the *Language to install, Time and currency format,* and *Keyboard or input method* settings, if necessary, and click Next.

4. Click Install Now. The *Type your product key for activation* page appears.

5. Clear the Automatically activate Windows when I'm online check box and click Next without typing a product key. An Install Windows message box appears, prompting you to enter a product key.

6. Click No. The *Select the edition of Windows that you purchased* page appears.

7. Select Windows Vista Enterprise. Then select the I have selected the edition of Windows that I purchased check box and click Next. The *Please read the license terms page* appears.

8. Select the I accept the license terms check box and click Next. The *Which type of installation do you want?* page appears.

9. Click Custom (advanced). The *Where do you want to install Windows?* page appears.

 If there are existing partitions on the computer's hard disk, select each one in turn and delete it before proceeding.

10. Select Disk 0 Unallocated Space and click Next. The *Installing Windows* page appears, indicating the progress of the Setup program as it installs the operating system. After the installation completes and the computer restarts, the *Choose a name and picture* page appears.

11. In the *Type a user name* text box, type **Student**.

12. In the *Type a password* and *Retype your password* text boxes, type **Pa$$w0rd**.

13. In the *Type a password hint* text box, type **Student** and click Next. The *Type a computer name and choose a desktop background* page appears.

14. In the *Type a computer name* text box, type **NYC-CLx**, where **x** is a unique number on the network. Then click Next. The *Help protect windows automatically* page appears.

15. Click *Ask me later*. The *Review your time and date settings* page appears.

16. If the time zone is not correct for your location, select the correct zone in the *Time zone* drop-down list.

17. If the time and/or date shown are not correct, set the correct date and time and click Next. The *Set your computer's current location* page appears.

18. Click Work. The *Thank you* page appears.

19. Click Start. The *Windows logon* page appears.

20. Log on using the Student account and the password Pa$$w0rd. The *Welcome Center* window appears.

21. Click Show more details. The System control panel appears.

> *If the System control panel does not indicate that Service Pack 1 or higher has been installed with Windows Vista, then you must install the Service Pack yourself on each workstation before allowing the students to use them.*

22. Leave the workstation logged on.

Joining a Workstation to a Domain

Overview	After installing Windows Vista, you must join the workstation to your network's Active Directory Domain Services domain.
Completion time	10 minutes

1. Click Start. Then click Control Panel. The *Control Panel* window appears.

2. Click System and Security > System. The *System* control panel appears.

3. Click Change settings. The *System Properties* sheet appears.

4. Click Change. The *Computer Name/Domain Changes* dialog box appears.

5. Select the Domain option, and type **contoso** in the text box. Then click OK. A *Windows Security* dialog box appears.

6. Authenticate with the username **Administrator** and the password **Pa$$w0rd** and click OK. A message box appears, welcoming you to the domain.

7. Click OK. Another message box appears, prompting you to restart the computer.

8. Click OK.

9. Click Close to close the *System Properties* dialog box.

10. A *You must restart your computer to apply these changes* message box appears.

11. Click Restart Now. The computer restarts.